The Millennium Book

Of
Self-Discovery

*A route map for the turn of the century leading towards
a new prosperity,
an enrichment of life, and the discovery of
the real you!*

Allen Carmichael
*Author of 'Believe you can!'
and 'The Small Book of Personal Growth'*

C O N C E P T (England)

"MULTI-LEVEL MARKETING"

ISBN 1 873288 00 X   *Concept* - July 1990

"NETWORK & MULTI-LEVEL MARKETING" (retitled 2nd edition)

ISBN 1 873288 01 8   *Concept* - September 1991

            Reprinted - June 1993   April 1994 (with additions)

            September 1995 - Revised and re-designed 3rd edition

            ISBN 1 873288 14 X

"BELIEVE YOU CAN!"

ISBN 1 873288 03 4   *Concept* - November 1992

"FOUR-SQUARE-SELLING"

ISBN 1 873288 04 2   *Concept* - Autumn 1994

"THE NETWORK MARKETING SELF-STARTER"

ISBN 1 873288 02 6   *Concept* - November 1991

Second edition - August 1994

"THE ULTIMATE GOAL"

ISBN 1 873288 19 0

Concept November 1995

Reprinted February 1996

"THE SMALL BOOK OF PEERSONAL GROWTH

ISBN 1 873288 24 7

Concept October 1998

Second edition - June 1999 - ISBN 1 873288 29 8

© *Concept* 1998 'THE MILLENIUM BOOK OF SELF-DISCOVERY'

All rights reserved. No part of this publication may be reproduced, stored in a retrieval system or transmitted in any form or by any means, electronic, mechanical, photocopying, recording or otherwise without prior permission of the copyright holders.

ISBN 1 873288 34 4

Concept - October 1999

        Printed in Finland by Werner Soderstrom Oy

   Published by *CONCEPT(England) . PO Box 614 . Polegate . East Sussex . BN26 5SS*

   Telephone/Fax 01323 485434   E-mail: sales@conceptengland.freeserve.co.uk

        Www.conceptengland.freeserve.co.uk

Contents

	Introduction	1
1	Point of departure...	11
2	Take a look at yourself	15
3	Motivation and society	25
4	The power of the subconscious	37
5	Seeking change	51
6	Who is in charge?	57
7	Dynamic Energy - *DE*	69
8	Peaks and troughs	75
9	Goals, targets & recognition	79
10	False limitations	91
11	Winners and losers	99
12	Success	107
13	Change - and the power of the unseen	117
14	Desire, belief and expectation	129
15	Planning and rehearsal	141
16	The habit of success	147
17	The final move!	161
18	Conclusion	165
	Appendix 1 - Obesity	169
	Appendix 2 - Smoking	177
	Appendix 3 - Redundancy	183
	Appendix 4 - Coincidence	189

'Sometimes a book...taken up at random,
merely with the object of reading it as a pastime,
has been known to call forth energies whose existence
had not before been suspected.'
- *Samuel Smiles 1859*

Introduction

It is always the same. Every New Year we resolve to make changes - changes to ourselves and changes to our surroundings. But where do we start? After reading this book, you will be in no doubt as to where or how, or indeed *why* you should start, nor indeed, where such beginnings may take you!

New Year resolutions have a way of following a set pattern. We begin in all sincerity, intending to become better people through whatever resolutions we may set ourselves, but somehow all the bright new thoughts and habits have a way of dwindling away, like sand slipping through our fingers. This does not mean we are weak and feeble, unable to keep to our well-intentioned promises. It simply means *we are human!*

It also probably means that we launched into our resolutions without a lot of thought, and with insufficient preparation.

Since we make resolutions at every new year, surely the turn of a century suggests that we should make some extra special effort towards new beginnings. Psychologically, the arrival of a new millenium is the perfect time for us to take ourselves seriously, assess our potential and to start making the profound adjustments that will affect all we do.

And we cannot start the process of change and development too soon.

Begin your life-planning now and resolve that things are going to start going your way...

My book *'Believe you can!'* was a by-product of observations of my own behaviour and experience under very stressful and unexpected circumstances. Out of the traumas

INTRODUCTION

and dramas I encountered, I evolved, not without the help of others, a philosophy of belief that was the basis of my recovery, and indeed the start of a completely new career.

Since writing that book I have had time to think about it's content and re-evaluate many of the book's themes, and, as a result, I came to the conclusion there was a lot more I would like to have said on the whole subject of self discovery. I therefore decided to re-appraise and rewrite *'Believe you can!'* in a new edition. The outcome of this exercise - rather than being the intended rewrite - is a virtually new volume which I felt, under the circumstances, deserved a new title - hence *'The Millenium Book of Self-Discovery'*.

I cannot claim any special qualifications for the production of this book. It is, like the original *'Believe you can!'*, simply the product of my own observations - of both myself and of those around me, and the interaction between the two.

Most of us would probably admit that life has not brought us everything we would have wished. This is really nobody's fault but our own. Most likely there were things we should have done, as well as things we would rather forget that we ever did. However, there was never anything to be gained by dwelling on things past and gone - speculating on the *what-might-have-been*. The possibility and potential for both change, adjustment, and improvement is something of which we are all aware, but, following the fault lines, how many of us are prepared to make the effort to improve our situation?

And yet, change is a possibility available to all of us, and certainly something from which everyone of us could benefit. All that is required to set things in motion is the firm decision to be part of the solution, rather than part of the problem.

INTRODUCTION

This, then, is to be a book about change, achievement, and fulfilment, and about the possibilities available to the open-minded adventurer prepared to penetrate the farthest corners of life in the quest for success, personal growth, and self-satisfaction.

But just what *is* success? Simply put, it is *the accomplishment of aims*, and the *achievement of goals*. It is a very personal thing, however, relative to individual circumstances and personal aspirations. Our perception of our own success may not always relate to that which we see in other people. What constitutes success varies from person to person, so it would be useful to consider just where you feel it lies in your own life. It can be all things to all men - is it, for example, the attainment of great wealth? Is it the achievement of long-standing ambitions? Is it a desire to become a better person? Is it a wish to become more spiritual?

It might be all of these things - or none of them. It may be little more than a sensation, a scarcely tangible entity or a continuing experience which grows and develops, fed by the adrenalin that it itself produces. At times it is something we can actually see and measure. Sometimes it is no more than a sense of well-being from which we may benefit by association. It may be the rosy glow of self-satisfaction at the achievement of something that to others might appear quite trivial and scarcely worth pursuing. Success is not a point at which one suddenly arrives - it is a journey rather than a destination. One may, for a moment, feel success has arrived when a goal is achieved - but it never takes long for us to realise that there is always something more beyond, another goal, another target that will inevitably push forward the boundary we thought we had drawn around ourselves.

As human beings we are surprisingly vulnerable, and this is one of our fundamental and endearing charms. We

INTRODUCTION

are, each one of us, completely alone, accountable to ourselves for our actions. No matter how high we may climb, or with what visible symbols and tokens of success we may choose to surround ourselves, beneath the surface we are all very much the same - vulnerable to insecurities and worries, and exposed to the same strokes of fate and fortune. *It is the way we handle these common problems and the manner in which we acquit ourselves that secures our position in the success stakes.*

Human beings are extraordinarily resilient and have a vast capacity for both revival and survival. Just as well in this unreliable world of ours, made up, as it is, of peaks and troughs, our time metered by a swinging pendulum that can carry us from success to failure in a remarkably short span of time.

When I wrote *'Believe you can!'* I quoted a statistic from Dunn & Bradstreet (March 1992), the business statisticians, which reported that in Britain 160 small businesses were collapsing each and every day! How terrible that sounded when reported, almost gleefully, by a news media obsessed - as it was at that time - with prophecies of doom and gloom, conveniently omitting to point out the number of new businesses that were *launched* over the same period. The fact that hundreds may have failed in one particular field has never been seen as any sort of deterrent to others from believing they could succeed at the very same thing! Thank goodness we *are* like that! Happily, since *'Believe you can!'* first appeared, the general economic situation has taken a firm and definite up-turn. Recession, like a super tanker, rolls forward with a momentum that takes a lot of stopping. Recovery, in the same way, is bound to be slow and ponderous.

INTRODUCTION

As I have said, this book is dedicated to the concept of success and achievement, and to the concept of change. If we want our situation to change, *it is we who must change first.* You may feel dissatisfied with the person you perceive yourself to be. That should be no great surprise - most of us feel the same way. You may dislike your situation and grumble at the circumstances you think have created it. Again, not at all an uncommon feeling. You may have been a victim of redundancy and seen the termination of a career path you imagined yourself treading for ever. Whatever the circumstances, they do not have to continue as a burden - they *can* be discarded, altered and rearranged to suit new challenges. But these things can only be brought about by setting in motion the machinery that will create *personal* change - and that means *change in you.*

We all tend to surround ourselves with patterns of behaviour that have a way of constantly repeating. Some years ago, when interviewing candidates for a job, I was always keen to identify patterns - and they could usually be uncovered without too much difficulty. For example, if an interviewee made constant reference to not seeing eye to eye with management, it was not unreasonable to assume that such a pattern would continue to repeat itself with any new employer. Such patterns represent the yardsticks for potential success or failure.

As we trail through life each of us carries a great deal of excess baggage. Change is as much a matter of *discarding and rejecting* as of acquiring anything new. Travelling light adds so much more appeal to the prospect of a journey. That tedious adage about not being able to teach an old dog new tricks is another thing that should be dumped in the bin along

INTRODUCTION

with all the other garbage, for that is where it belongs! The old dog must be shown how to discard its own threadbare tricks, and be given something better and more productive to do with its time!

New beginnings have frequently been the direct result of an adverse situation. It is easy, through complacency, to allow oneself to slide imperceptibly into a life of comforting and boring routine - and it has often been said that the difference between a rut and a grave is merely a matter of depth. Within routine lies what might often appear to be security, but modern life can so easily demonstrate the folly of that particular assumption. We live in times where the unexpected is a constant happening - and has indeed almost become the expected. No longer is it safe to assume that bad news is something that only affects other people. Job-loss, redundancy and business collapse are no longer exceptional occurrences. But, being commonplace does not invalidate the devastating affects of these sombre happenings on the individual. To have one's life suddenly disturbed and disrupted could never be described as either pleasant nor desirable. Yet, in a curious way, these events may actually have value in the wider scheme of things. They could be the trigger needed to jerk us out of our comfortable complacency and make us aware of latent skills we had forgotten, which could be used to create new and fascinating opportunities.

To attempt to bring about change or modification we need to understand the factors that have helped to mould us and make us the people we are. Each one of us is the sum total of everything that has happened to us so far in life. We are encrusted with layer upon layer of habit and inherited concepts. We have been shaped and honed by influences over which we had little choice or control, as well as by

INTRODUCTION

circumstances that we created ourselves, intentionally or otherwise. If modification is the requirement, *we do need to know exactly what to modify!* As human beings we are, as I have said, very adaptable, but only providing we are in control. However, there are times when control has been allowed to slip away, permitting other people and other circumstances to dictate events. It is vital that every human being keeps control of his or her own situation. Only through this can we hope to achieve anything.

Most actions and their consequences are the outcome of mental attitudes, therefore some understanding of the mechanics of our minds - in simple terms - puts us in possession of a tool of considerable value.

I have already said that patterns tend to repeat themselves. But this is only true up to a point, for patterns, if the will to change them is there, can be disturbed and altered. Change, however, is only feasible when two vital ingredients are present. The most important of these is the *desire* for change, and the other, the *belief that change is possible.*

So, given those two requirements - desire for and belief in change - it *is* possible to modify ourselves. By setting such a process in motion, we begin to re-evaluate our surroundings, which in their turn are also going to change - or, more precisely, it is our perception of our immediate environment that will change. We need, therefore, to create a personal plan for survival. It is then up to each of us to use the building blocks of that plan to seek, recognise, evaluate and exploit the new opportunities life will most certainly put on offer.

Some people see their lives as being filled with problems and difficulties - but no problem is insurmountable - *there is always a solution.* Difficulties are simply stumbling blocks

INTRODUCTION

which have to be faced and overcome by working through them. There is nothing that, when approached with logic and reason, cannot be conquered.

My own particular voyage of discovery was activated by being made redundant - of which more later - certainly circumstances that could not be described as being of my own choosing. Through these dramatic and unpleasant circumstances I unearthed a whole new career, travelling a bumpy road along which I learned a great deal that I now consider worth passing on to others in the hope they, too, may discover that the light at the end of their own particular tunnel is not, after all, an on-coming train!

I may not have found the complete answer, because anything that can be described as a journey of self-improvement never actually has a point of termination. And, of course, nothing that I write can turn you into someone else - not even *you* can do that for yourself. The best I can hope to do is to present you with certain ideas and concepts that may lead you along a number of different paths which will provide you with directional choice, as you initiate your personal search for the things you want out of life.

Any book of this nature can be no more than a starting point - the particular direction you take will reveal itself to you as your exploration of yourself unfolds. To quote a pertinent truism - *when the student is ready, the teacher will appear.*

This business of change and modification is a mysterious process which must be approached with a completely open mind. There is no room for scepticism or doubt. If you feel change of any sort is a desirable goal in your life, for whatever reason, don't push too hard, rather allow yourself

INTRODUCTION

to be *lead* towards it. I have no doubt whatsoever that along the way you will make some fascinating discoveries. All I ask is that you allow this book to be your starting point, never your ultimate solution!

Believe in your aims and in yourself, and in the idea that it is possible to set a chain of events in motion that you have not totally planned. All the answers lie *within you*, so let your watchword be... *awareness*.

Allen Carmichael - September 1999

1
Point of departure...

Starting points are always tricky and always problematic... Starting to write a book is difficult in itself. Unless you have experienced it, it is unlikely that you would appreciate just how many decisions have to be made, even before pen is put to paper. But, thank goodness, the starting point for any form of self-improvement is total simplicity, for all that is involved in creating the blue touch-paper for ignition is one simple thing - *desire.*

Desire is the *motivation,* the very driving force of life.

And motivation is such an emotive word! Motivation is involved in every aspect of our daily lives. We all experience emotional ups and downs - the tragedies, triumphs and disappointments - for they are the peaks and troughs, the hills and valleys of the landscape of life. We go through periods of indecision, times when we lack all sense of direction. It is on these occasions that a greater understanding of how we tick - what in fact *motivates* us - and more importantly, how *we could be made to tick more effectively*, could be of immense value.

I was very aware as I wrote *'Believe you can!'* that a vast diversity of people would eventually buy the book - people from all walks of life, following all manner of occupations, but with one thing in common - all of them looking for *something.* From the feedback *Concept England),* my publishers, received, this proved to be exactly the case. The Australian edition of *'Believe you can!'* had much the same effect on people and the book quickly achieved best-seller status in that country. It also became the focal point for a national television programme on self-help.

It soon became clear that my readers were approaching the idea of change and new beginnings from a variety of angles, for a diversity of different reasons, and with varying degrees of expectation - and, not least of all, *scepticism.*

There will be many people who pick up this book and find some of the ideas it puts forward very difficult to accept. This is of no consequence, for it is possible that the book may sow a small seed that will, given time, grow and develop in a scrap of fertile soil in the same way that a fern can take root on a stone wall. All I would ask of you, the reader, is that you keep an open mind as you read. My guess is that, since you have bought the book, you *are* looking for answers - and as I said in my introduction, the answers already lie within you. The most I can do is provide the key that may unlock a creaky door or two.

One man who wrote to me said that the book contained nothing he didn't already know - but, to use his own words, *'...it provided the needed kick up the backside'* that literally changed his life! I am not offering instant solutions, for really there are none. What I hope is that we, you and I, may travel an interesting road together and, whilst doing that, may achieve some sort of *resonance.* Zen Buddhists describe resonance by pointing out that if a violin is lying unattended in a room in which the 'A' note is struck on a tuning fork, the 'A' string on the violin will vibrate and be heard quite clearly from across the room. But you would have to listen carefully - *you would have to be in a state of expectant awareness.*

This journey we are about to undertake is not related to anything specific in the way of circumstances or occupation. We are concerned with ideas and concepts that can fit any

POINT OF DEPARTURE...

situation. If we can begin to understand *why we are what we are,* there is hope that we may be able to unpick a few of the knots and re-tie them in some new, improved, more significantly interesting way.

The generality of the ideas I want to present to you will satisfy most people, whilst others may feel the need to know much more and delve deeper into many of the notions I want to hand on to you. This, of course, is excellent, because a book of this nature can only touch on things, many of which really deserve much more space, much more detail. It is up to the individual reader to take what is useful and to carry on his or her own more detailed and personal exploration of the things that are of particular significance. There are so many excellent books covering every aspect of self-development.

To please all of the people all of the time is, most probably, a vain and presumptuous expectation!

Some years ago an American architect was commissioned to design a new department store on the west coast of the United States. He began by visiting the proposed site and wandering over the terrain until he reached its highest point where he sat down to admire the spectacular view. It soon became obvious to him that where he was sitting had to be a place where people would wish to relax and linger, to admire the prospect he presently found so pleasing - in fact this very spot had to be the site for the store's restaurant. So he took out his sketch pad and designed the cover for the book of matches that would eventually be on the tables!

The whole concept for the building developed and blossomed outwards from that simple beginning, that first step of commitment, to become a unified and cohesive whole. Whatever we are hoping to achieve, we all need to find our

POINT OF DEPARTURE...

own particular starting point. Every journey, no matter how long and arduous, starts with just one single step...
...*commitment.*

Positive action:

1. Make a declaration to yourself *now* that you are committed to the idea of bettering your circumstances in any way you can, both spiritually and materially Decide that you are prepared to do what ever is necessary to create change and bring added value to the quality of your own life and of those around you. Write down *why* you have decided on this course of action.

2. Write down your *feelings* about this in detail - *as a declaration of intent.*

3. On the basis that *you could not fail,* write down *everything* you would like to achieve or acquire in life. Keep these notes in a file, dated, for we will return to this again later on.

2
Take a look at yourself...

Take heart! - do not be afraid.
Look about you and seek opportunity...

When, I wonder, did you last review your circumstances or evaluate your situation? Get out a sheet of paper or a pad and write down these four questions...

> Where have I come from?
> Where am I right now?
> Where am I going?
> What have I done so far to ensure I get there?

Obviously, the next thing to do is to answer the questions one by one. I would like you to do this exercise right now - being totally honest with yourself. This is the starting point for our voyage of self-discovery and revelation. Write down your answers in as much detail as possible *before you read any further.*

Don't cheat on yourself! - leave turning this page until you have completed this exercise to your entire satisfaction...

TAKE A LOOK AT YOURSELF

Looking at your answers you may realise that *where you have come from* is not perhaps as relevant to the purposes of this exercise as *where you are now,* since this is the direct result of choices you already made in the past. But what do you *now* feel about the outcome of those decisions?...

- Are you satisfied?
- Did you in fact make the right choices?
- Was it a difficult route you travelled?
- Were all the options easy?
- Do you feel happy and fulfilled with the way things have turned out?

Is life still offering challenge, or has the excitement been replaced by apparently unalterable routine? Do you feel you are the victim of circumstances over which you believe you have little or no control? *Does the future seem to offer anything more than an endless sameness, drifting away into the misty distance?*

Every day is filled with choices. If your present situation is the result of choices you made in the past, it is logical to assume that you may shape and develop your future by the choices available to you now.

Ask yourself this simple question: *how much money did you earn over the past ten years?* When you have worked out the sum, the next question is: *how much of that money do you have now?*

It is quite a salutary experience to realise what a lot of money has passed through your hands, for which you now have virtually nothing to show. The interesting outcome of

TAKE A LOOK AT YOURSELF

this simple but revealing exercise is to project your likely earnings over the *next* ten years and decide how you may make provision to ensure that at least some of it is saved for your own future economic security - and the satisfaction of, at least, having something to show for your labours.

Precisely similar thoughts can apply to life in general. How well did you use the past ten years, and what have you got to show for it...?

Doesn't this make you realise how vitally important it is to spend some time over the choices and decisions that could be made *now* which will have profound repercussions on the next ten years - *and, indeed, on the rest of your life?*

So...where *are* you going?   Have you made any choices or decisions? If you haven't, the likelihood is that your life will drift on in its unexciting way until you reach its inevitable conclusion.   That may sound somewhat depressing - it is not intended to!   It is intended to encourage you to be realistic. There is no point in pussyfooting about with life - you cannot relive time that has passed, and there will be no action replay. It is like parachuting or bungy jumping - there are no rehearsals, you have to get it right the first time!   That is not to say that second chances in life are not a possibility.   You obviously cannot alter the past, but you are in a position to reshape and modify the future.

'Where are you going', of course, can only be related to decisions of a purely temporary nature - unless you have a totally rigid plan which offers no possibility of deviation, come what may.   If your thinking *is* like that, I am afraid you have got it wrong again, because allowing no possibility

TAKE A LOOK AT YOURSELF

for deflection, change, or deviation is simply a recipe for disaster.

Georges Braque, the French painter, when talking about creativity, used to say that if it was possible to visualise a finished picture in one's mind with such clarity, certainty and vividness that all one had to do was to put it down on canvas, the result would be worthless and uninteresting. He contended that the hand of creativity would not have touched such a work. He believed fervently that a painter must approach everything with a totally open mind, since it is the *exploitation of the accidental* that is the true basis of all creativity. The painter may well set out with a vivid mental picture of what he intends to paint, but inevitably things will happen on the journey towards that goal which may totally alter his intention, and at this exciting moment - the moment when true creativity takes charge - produce results far beyond expectation or the original visualisation. This then is the nature of creativity.

As we travel through life we are constantly faced with forks in the road, choices between two possible directions. Important decisions have to be made, but without going into the exact nature of these decisions, there is a simple rule of thumb one can apply...

Providing one always selects the more difficult option, there will rarely be cause for regret in the future.

The easy option, though tempting and perhaps temporarily fulfilling, rarely leads to any permanent satisfaction.

In examining *where you are now,* did you take the scenic route of easy options to bring you to your present

TAKE A LOOK AT YOURSELF

situation? Or did you travel the more difficult, rugged and challenging route? Ask yourself this:

If you had it all to do again, would you make any changes?

Until now, have you ever thought seriously about the possibility of change in your life? Have you considered the idea that you could be the master of your own destiny? Has it ever struck you that, no matter what a shambles your life may have become, with little of note by way of achievement, there is *still* unlimited opportunity for real and lasting success to be yours?

The possibility is always available and lies very much within your grasp, requiring only the one thing I have already mentioned to set the process of change in motion - *desire*. It is for you to take the decision that could make your *reach* exceed your *grasp*. Nobody can push you as far as you can push yourself. Success must be *planned and anticipated.* It is never going to spring out of the wardrobe and take you by surprise.

There is one more powerful question to ask yourself at this stage. Does your present job, assuming you have one, *have the potential to alter your future?*

What, indeed, would you ask of that future? If you could start again, are there aspects of your life you would choose to alter? Everyone should have dreams...but, so far, how close has the reality of your life come to those dreams?

Stop for a moment to consider the following questions...

- Do you have dreams and aspirations?
- If the choice was yours, where, ideally, would you like to live?

TAKE A LOOK AT YOURSELF

- What car would you like to drive?
- How do you visualise your ideal lifestyle?

This book is not intended to be a textbook or a training manual. The idea is that *you* do the work! The book is there in your hands to encourage you to explore yourself, ask questions of yourself, and even question the answers you will find. The book will not answer the questions for you. What it *should* do is to act merely as a prompt to make you think.

Since writing *'Believe you can!'* Concept has had some interesting responses from people whose lives have literally been transformed, people who have picked themselves up and made a new start. The most common comment has been along the lines that ...*yes, I knew what had to be done! But I needed someone to give me a real reason for doing it!*

The book is a starting point for your own effort. You may find, so long as you remain open and receptive, it will lead you towards some odd and unexpected experiences. It should help to clarify future moves and point out the route you should follow. Attempts to stimulate the processes of change can, and sometimes do, result in strange and bizarre experiences, but these are merely part of the learning curve. Learn from everything, look for the reason behind, or meaning for, every experience, be prepared for the unexpected and be ready to respond to the ideas and hunches that may come to you. Remember the process of creativity - *to recognise and exploit the accidental or the unexpected.*

Always be *aware* and *awake* to the messages that your actions will arouse in you - sometimes as dreams, sometimes as sudden flashes of inspiration, sometimes as strong hunches. Always take notice of such things, and be ready to act on them, if necessary, for these are the signals from your subconscious, the directional and instructional indicators that

TAKE A LOOK AT YOURSELF

are part of the fascinating process of literally *waking up*. So, always aim to be alert and responsive, for life will surely confront you with surprises and reward you for your efforts.

It doesn't matter how old you are, it is never too late to create change and strive towards new goals. Hopefully, it will not be long before you are asking yourself why on earth you didn't do something like this years ago? The fact is *you didn't* - and looking over your shoulder never achieved anything worthwhile, so put worthless thoughts like that out of your mind. It could be, of course, that you were not ready for the process until now. It is strange how often in life that - to quote the Buddhist saying again - *when the pupil is ready, the teacher appears.*

Make a resolution right here and now that the time has gone when you were inclined to wait for things to happen - from this point on you are going to be in charge - and in a position *to make them happen!*

Do you ever have the thought that some people are luckier than others? Take a look at the people you consider to be lucky. Could it be that the luckiest people you know also happen to be the most active and industrious? They will almost certainly be people who go out and make things happen. Can you see how they create their own good fortune through their attitude? Such happenings are often attributed to good luck - but it is no real surprise to note how good luck so often attends the efforts of the most industrious people!

On meeting a writer or a painter - or any creative person - there is a tendency to assume that theirs is a wonderful life in which work is only necessary - or indeed possible - when inspiration strikes. If this was really the case, not a great

TAKE A LOOK AT YOURSELF

deal would get done! Very few creative people would survive for long! This elusive thing we call inspiration often has to be prised from its hiding place by sheer hard work - in other words, by creating the right circumstances, the fertile ground in which the frail plant may grow and flourish.

Forcing the pace by pushing hard, even though nothing of worth seems to be happening *at that moment* can create the circumstances where, quite suddenly, out of the strife and effort, the spark appears that ignites the creative fire. There is nothing magical about this. It is simply the manifestation of what I call *Dynamic Energy (DE)*. This is a wonderful phenomenon that we all experience in varying degrees in practically every aspect of our lives - a potent mix of sheer enjoyment, inspiration and excitement which allows us to emerse ourselves totally in any activity to the exclusion of all outside distractions, whilst, at the same time, providing the necessary energy and drive to see a task through. It is the pinnacle and the reward for having developed true *awareness*. I intend to devote a whole chapter to *DE* later in the book.

Positive action:

1. Did you answer the four initial questions on the first page of this chapter. Even though you may not have done, and have read the rest of the chapter, do answer them now! - and do it in detail! This is quite important.

2. Did you fully answer the questions on page 14? The starting point when seeking information is to first write down the questions - then the possible answers in detail.

3. Do these answers suggest any directional pointers? Have you a clearer idea of the way you should be facing?

TAKE A LOOK AT YOURSELF

4. Make another list! This time write down all your personal achievements. List all the occasions on which you really felt you had done extremely well - the situations that represented success in your own eyes.

5. Now do the same with your failures. List all the occasions when you felt you had truly failed. This is quite difficult and requires a degree of honesty. But it is well worth doing, for these are the things we tend to push deep down into our subconscious and try to forget. Bringing ghosts out into the open again in a deliberate way has the effect of minimising, or sometimes, completely dispelling them.

3
Motivation and society

The word *motive* is often defined as *'moving or impelling power'*, or *'a form of mechanical energy used to drive machinery'*. A *motive* is also that which induces a person to act. *Desire, fear,* or simply *circumstance,* are all examples of motive. To motivate, then, is to supply a motive and motivation could be described as supplying a reason for the performance of some action, often related to a specific goal.

There are, as with so many things in life, two sides to motivation, a positive and a negative. It has been suggested that the more intelligent a person is, the easier it is to motivate them. If this is true, it is perhaps because motivation requires imagination, and there is certainly a quantifiable relationship between intelligence and imagination.

We could apply a scale to intelligence, one end of it related to imagination, interest and a need for activity, whilst the other end would be concerned with fear, insecurity and, above all, *boredom* - that supreme negative, so prized by many of the less intelligent members of our society. Boredom and intelligence rarely go hand in hand.

In considering this negative side of motivation, you may well wonder where *fear* enters the equation. Is fear an extreme example of ignorance - or could it be the other way around? Fear of the unknown is a common manifestation of insecurity that comes through a lack of knowledge and understanding. Once fear is in place, anger is only a few paces away, for fear born out of ignorance is a dangerous emotion. It is so easy to make false assumptions when confronted with fear. It is then just as easy to take that assumption, doing nothing to check its viability or truth, and build on it until a situation becomes so distorted that violence appears to be the only possible outcome. This is the basis of much criminal behaviour - an obvious example, the crime of passion. But consider the dangerous implications that arise when such feelings occur in a *group* context. A group can take on a persona of its own, and, under this influence, human beings are inclined to act collectively in a way that none of them would consider reasonable individually.

The power of *group dynamics* can be quite awesome. By way of example, take football hooliganism - a classic situation where fear, born out of a degree of ignorance, mixed with raw emotion, and the excitement of the occasion, can reach epidemic proportions. Add to this potent cocktail, boredom, and you have the recipe for civil unrest, possibly on a grand scale.

Fear can take many forms. We all know about *fear of failure* - but that is only one manifestation. It is fear that can lead the under-achiever into deliberately seeking undemanding jobs because that individual has an actual - though unconscious - *fear of success.* A person, acting under the influence of such a fear, may even seek out very difficult jobs so that they cannot possibly be blamed if, as they expect, they will eventually fail.

Fear of success is usually very deeply rooted, often the result of an unconscious and unresolved feeling of guilt, prompted by an imagined worry over the prospect of beating, and therefore possibly eclipsing, one's own parent in some competitive sense. Strange are the workings of the mind.

It is all too common these days to hear the droning moans of youngsters - *its b-o-r-i-n-g,* or, *I'm soooo b-o-r-e-d.* These dull, uninspired whines are often the resort of personalities caught, through no actual fault of their own, in a modern social trap. The person constantly complaining of boredom is unconsciously experiencing a lack of discipline that could actually represent freedom. This may sound a contradiction in terms, but in discipline lies security, the state necessary to on-going happiness and freedom of thought. When there is a lack of discipline - and this is likely to be the result of a lack of parental responsibility - the bored adolescent no longer makes any effort to choose and control the direction that his or her life could be taking. There is an unwillingness for the young person also to accept *responsibility*. This sad attitude often gives rise to a chain reaction of negative emotions through which they will blame everything *external* for their many problems, without ever admitting, or even acknowledging the obvious fact that it is their own attitude that is actually at fault. This is why it is so necessary to understand that, if we are dissatisfied with our surroundings and have the desire for change, *it is we that must first change.*

Young people - and we can see this particularly in areas of severe unemployment or deprivation - can too easily create a breeding ground for negative thoughts and emotions. They tend to hang around in groups, collectively complaining about the way the world is treating them, how rotten their parents are to them, and how lousy their teachers are (or were) to them. Feeding one another, they pile negative upon negative, producing a thick dark cloud of demotivation which progressively envelops them. What I find especially worrying today is that we may have produced a generation of youngsters who will carry the scars of their own self-inflicted negativism into later life - eventually affecting future generations. This can only lead to a steady degeneration at the lower end of our social scale which could, given the right circumstances, affect the whole of our society.

What has gone wrong? It seems to come down to one or two simple factors. The first is that discipline has become totally eroded in those specific areas in which it had the greatest benefit - home and school. Where is the discipline in a school in which the staff exist in a permanent state of fear or anxiety, worried about the reaction of pupils, their parents, and even legislative authority, should they see fit to punish a child? We are constantly being told that the quality of teaching, especially in state schools, has dropped. Teachers have difficulty in maintaining order, and in capturing the imagination of their classes. There is often a noticeable lack of leadership and direction from the people who should be providing the motivation to return school life to a state of enjoyment and learning, rather than a constant battle against authority.

One might hope that public opinion - outraged by this state of affairs - would demand immediate solutions to be sought for such problems - but no! The whole point is - and this attitude, I believe, pervades our national life at this time - *nobody wants to take responsibility for anything.*

The young person is not necessarily responsible for being knocked down by these shortcomings, but they *are* responsible, often, for *not doing anything about getting up...*

You may feel we have strayed somewhat from the subject of *motivation* - but surely, we are on the right track, for that is the missing ingredient that lies behind all these problems. What is missing is the motivation or, more precisely, *the desire* to do something about reinstating an attitude of responsibility, for bringing back sufficient discipline to impart a much-needed sense of security - a sense of actually *belonging.* Human beings respond so well when they have a sense of direction, and it is exactly that which discipline imparts to people who have been left to flounder. Children actually unconsciously *crave* for discipline as it provides them with the feelings of security so necessary to their development. When discipline has been reinstated, perimeters have been drawn, the line has been scratched in the sand beyond which one must not venture. Parents, teachers, social workers, the media - and indeed, every one of us - should start examining their own very specific role in the process of stopping the rot that is leading so clearly towards the development of an under-class. All too often the majority turn their backs and shuffle embarrassedly towards a new fence on which to sit, rather than make any commitment towards bettering the situation.

What we have been discussing is the nature of motivation in all its worst forms. One can understand how a person may feel trapped in what appears to be a no-hope situation, influenced, as they can so easily be, by the negative attitudes of other people. There is no leader and no follower in such a context, so it is down to the individual to make the supreme effort to break out of the circle and *accept responsibility for themselves,* believing totally in their ability to restart their own life. Rarely will people admit that the blame for their situation lies within themselves, as the product and result of their own attitudes. It is so much easier to blame outside agencies for their misfortunes, because this way, once again, *there is no need to feel any personal responsibility.*

Once an individual shows the willingness to take a long, serious look at his or her self and comes to the realisation that they are the cause of many of their own problems, they are truly on the road to taking control of their own lives. Then, they have the opportunity to put that first foot forward, to break out of the endless circle at the start of a journey that will release all the wonderful, dormant potential that lies buried deep within them.

In any large organisation within the corporate world, attitudes come from the top and spread downwards right through the pyramidal structure.

A positive boss, full of expectation as to the ability and efficiency of his employees, will have a successful and highly motivated work force. The employees, in their turn, will recognise that they have a boss for whom they enjoy working. He understands the needs of the people he employs, and is very aware of the importance of allowing (and encouraging) them to set their own goals, since, in the wider context, these will probably be much the same as his own goals for the prosperity of the company.

When goals are set by a superior, there is a danger of undermining feelings of personal responsibility. Personal motivation and self-esteem may become dented, with the inevitable outcome - resentment, and this is not an attitude anyone would consciously wish to promote within a working environment. To get the best out of employees, a good employer will allow personal freedom in the setting of goals and achievement of targets, and this feeling will be carried down through the various levels of management structure, eventually permeating the whole corporate structure. The outcome will be to ensure both company loyalty and personal job satisfaction. This attitude is born out of a fundamental human truth - *nobody minds being told what to do, but everyone dislikes being told how to do it!* All this achieves is to rob the individual of personal responsibility, not to mention denting their self-image.

MOTIVATION AND SOCIETY

There is always a reverse or negative side to such ideas. The critical, condemnatory, dogmatic employer is likely to generate attitudes of resentment and indifference among his staff, and this will colour the way in which all layers of management behave, passing potential failure down through the structure. The over authoritarian attitude can also be blamed for another unpleasant feature of employment - bullying. We hear a lot of talk about bullying in the corporate world, talk of people being intimidated by superiors to a point where they become completely dysfunctional and therefore of very little value to the organisation that employs them. At the very worst such cases have been known to actually result in suicide.

Bullying (and the attitudes that permit or in some extreme cases actually encourage such a syndrome) just like all other attitudes, emanate from the top - either by intent, or by default. Directors may be blindly unaware of what is happening within the corporate structure, or are not prepared to do anything to stamp out practices that they know exist and that are detrimental to the running of a successful business. Bullying is perhaps the most undermining problem that can occur within a company. It is a poison which can totally de-motivate a company, even to eventually developing into a destructive force working against the aspirations of that company.

The bully should have no place in any workforce. This is one area where to reprimand publicly is completely acceptable. Exposure and dismissal are the only ways to cut out this insidious block to corporate growth and progress, undermining as it does all hope of good relationships between workers and management.

I have been self-employed for the greater part of my working life, but I did for a short time work for a company which was quite young when I joined them. The whole organisation was enthused with the excitement of expectation. It was alive and buzzing with the electricity of positive anticipation that flooded down through the whole structure, from the board room to the post room. This was a company that could do nothing but succeed - and in the most dynamic way. From day one there was a system in operation at every level by which each individual had to produce a simple report on the person immediately below him or her, every month. In some organisations such a system could have been regarded as very negative, perceived almost as spying. But not in this case! It had the most positive effect and everyone recognised the added value it produced, causing real and personal feelings of responsibility towards the job. There was great corporate enthusiasm. The constant question asked was not *how* things could be done, but *why* things should be done. There was a questioning approach to problem solving in which everyone was encouraged to express opinions. Senior management demonstrated an acute awareness that the success of the company depended on the people they employed having the right attitude. The organisation became a company *that people wanted to work for.*

Any well run organisation knows the importance of *recognition* - that pat-on-the-back everyone needs from time to time. It demonstrates awareness of what an employee is doing, or has done, and in a small way also says thank you. It enhances feelings of expectation and of belief in that person. Acts like this may appear small and trivial - and that can often be the reason that they so easily get forgotten or neglected - but they really are of vital importance to the development and on-going enrichment of human relations. Anyone in authority who disregards such simple things, does so at his peril! Discipline, tempered by mutual respect, is not a difficult balance to achieve or maintain, providing one remembers a few simple rules. For example, *reprimand privately* and *praise publicly*, and be sure you understand the difference between *capability* and *effectiveness*. Real achievers are not the people who simply work to their capabilities, but the ones among us who combine effectiveness and the ability to sell their ideas to those around them. To maintain a high motivational level, it is important that the flow of goodwill operates in both directions.

Whilst good motivational attitudes usually emanate from the top and flow downwards through an organisation, it is often the case that ideas and concepts to improve efficiency are developed at the lower end of the scale, and pass upwards. Woe to the employer who disregards this or does not actively encourage creative and critical thinking. Nothing is more dispiriting to the employee than to have his ideas or suggestions swept aside or, worse, totally ignored. Yet there are many who fail to see the benefit of constantly testing the temperature of the water by listening to the workforce. The boss may have a reasonably clear vision - in broad brush terms - of the whole company scene, but it is the lower end of the corporate scale that often provides the fine brush strokes to complete the picture.

There is a curious situation that can occur within a company employing a direct sales force on a commission earning basis. Salaried directors have been known to become seriously resentful of salesmen who, through the commission earning system, make more money than they do. Any thinking employer should be delighted at such a state of affairs! - and be prepared to show his approval publicly. If, through commissions, every one of the sales team earned more than the managing director, the company would quickly be in such a buoyant state that the board could justify large salary increases for all its directors!

Positive action:
Ask yourself...

1. Have you ever given in to *boredom?* What effect did it have on you? Did you find the experience stimulating?

2. Have you ever allowed yourself to be drawn into a group of negative people? Did you join in the collective moaning? Did you derive any pleasure from the experience?

3. Have you ever allowed yourself to feel it just wasn't worth bothering to do something that might have affected the quality of your life, and the lives of those around you?

4. Have you ever felt you should do something about a situation that seemed wrong - then done nothing because you could not see how your small effort could have any effect?

5. If you are an employer, ask yourself, are you getting the most from your staff? Do you ever reward them over and above your obligations?

6. Are you a leader? Do you lead by *beckoning*

or by *pointing*? Consider this carefully. Is there room for any beneficial adjustment?

7. Ask yourself this - are you able to accept suggestions, criticisms and ideas from your employees? How much value do you place on their opinions?

8. Write down what you believe your employees think of you. Is your answer anything like the way in which you would hope to be thought of? Again, do you think you could make any beneficial adjustments?
If you are an employee, do the same exercise - but the other way around.

9. Are you good at motivating others? Could you honestly say you always recognise achievement in other people?

Resolve...
Never to associate again with negative people.
When you begin to feel bored, seek out the cause *and do something about it!*
Never allow yourself to be influenced in any way by people you do not admire.
Always maintain a positive attitude. There is no situation that does not have a possible positive solution.

Above all, *never imagine you know what other people are thinking.* This is a most dangerous practice. Realise that these are always *your* thoughts, *not theirs,* and, as such, can be very self-destructive - not to say *totally wrong, inaccurate and misleading!*

4
The power of the subconscious

Our brains operate on two main levels - the conscious and the sub-conscious. This is, of course, expressing amazingly complex pieces of human apparatus in the most simplistic way, but that is all I can presume to do as a mere layman. These two states are in constant communication, one with the other, sorting, making comparisons, assessing, evaluating, all to provide the continuous flow of data needed in our daily lives simply to enable us to make the decisions required to do everything we do to maintain a balance. A degree of understanding and appreciation of the manner in which this two-way flow operates will, I hope, be useful. There is one simple fact to constantly remember, expressed again in the most basic of terms, and that is that *the subconscious will believe everything it is told!*

The brain has often been likened to a computer - indeed, the computer is man's attempt to produce something as near to a human brain as he has been able to contrive. Man has now become so clever that we are told the latest generation of computers is so advanced as to be capable of out-pacing the human brain. The subconscious, like the computer, can manipulate any amount of information with which it is presented, and supply immediate feed-back to enable further decisions to be made, or actions to be taken.

If, for example, the subconscious receives the simple message...*'I am tired!'*...it will do everything to demonstrate and confirm the truth of this statement because it knows how and where to instantly find all the accumulated evidence of a lifetime on the subject of tiredness, carefully and meticulously stored in the filing system, and is able to produce it to completely justify the message it has received. Soon, not only are you feeling tired, but exhaustion begins to set in, slowly affecting all your functions, bringing everything to a halt!

Capacity - or the degree to which you experience anything - is a state of mind. Telling yourself you are exhausted will ensure you will feel just that! But, as with all things, there is a positive and a negative aspect to this. Energy is always available when you decide to do what *has* to be done - especially when it needs to be done *now!* Another odd thing is that when one's real interest is spontaneously aroused, feelings of tiredness dissipate in a flash, for the subconscious will have seized on this sudden new excitement and initiated a mini adrenalin rush to match the mood change and provide the necessary motivation to carry through the task.

Another example of the way the subconscious can affect your mood is worrying over the things you know you *should* have done but did not. Following this line of thought is totally non-productive, not to say a considerable drain on energy resources. The *what-might-have-been* syndrome is totally fruitless, just as the *if-only-I'd-done-this-years-ago* thought is equally pointless. The fact is *you didn't* - and that was probably because the time was not yet right and because you were not ready to make such a move!

In terms of energy, *immediacy* is the key that can release the supply. The subconscious is always ready - indeed, even anxious! - to spring into action at the slightest suspicion of a command, and, as we have seen, this can work in either direction, positively or negatively, for the subconscious will always do your bidding and follow the lead you initiate. The great lesson to learn here is that it is *you* who influences your subconscious - not the other way around. The role of the subconscious is that of continuous back-up.

'If you want something doing, ask a busy man.' Why do we so often say this? The answer is obvious, in the light of what we have just been discussing - the busy man is a *now* person, someone who derives his seemingly inexhaustible supply of energy from his habit of *immediate action.* He is usually a person well aware of the value and benefit of never putting off that which can be dealt with immediately. The creed by which such people live is *do it now!*

If you really desire to succeed, it is important to understand this philosophy, because putting things off is tantamount to giving your subconscious the opportunity to provide all the demotivational ideas that surround the notion of laziness. It is endowing the task with the label of *'unimportant'.*

Another over-worked adage is *'success breeds success'.* Perhaps, after the things we have just looked at, you can now see what this rather trite saying really means. What we are looking at is that fascinating cycle I have called *Dynamic Energy (DE).* *DE,* expressed simply, is the force that produces the adrenalin drive to get things done. It derives from a dynamic and excited interest, so obsessive that everything around it is precluded. *DE* is the consequence - the generated energy that has the power to attract both people as well as all manner of interesting possibilities - here, indeed, *is* success breeding success! The adrenalin that was instrumental in creating the initial drive that lead to some form of success, in turn produces its own extra adrenalin surge, driving one still further further towards achievement.

THE POWER OF THE SUBCONSCIOUS

The unsuccessful, lazy person, always ready with a fund of reasons and excuses for having done nothing, will spend as long telling you how busy they are as it might have taken to do the job they haven't the time to do! The difference with the successful person - the *now* person - is simply that he or she gets things done because they *have to be done,* and does not waste time telling you about it. Although this is essentially a matter of *attitude*, it demonstrates how important it is to realise that the subconscious is neither friend nor counsellor - it is a mechanism of startling complexity that is there to serve as your *servant.* You may utilise its astounding capacity in any way you choose. It will help you in equal measure in your quest for either success or failure. It is *you* that calls the tune, but it is your subconscious that plays it.

Attitude is of vital importance; it affects everything you do and say - and it can touch others just as easily as it will colour your own approach to life.

The world, it seems, is divided into *if/when* people and *now* people - and it requires only a small degree of adjustment to slide from one category towards the other - in either direction! If, for example, you are confronted with a task of dramatic proportions, don't waste time dwelling on the end result. Forget the difficulties that may appear to be there, and just concentrate on making a start - with immediate tasks and immediate action. Once the job is started, and a momentum has been generated, the route towards the job's conclusion will clearly define itself. It is amazing how the problems that seemed to beset the task will dissipate. This sort of approach is merely focusing on the *now* and the *here* - not agitating and stressing oneself with wasteful thoughts about difficulties and the final outcome of what one is doing.

THE POWER OF THE SUBCONSCIOUS

In sport this approach to the achievement of a goal is essential. Take the talented and aspiring tennis player. If he or she is told to concentrate on the goal of winning the *championship*, this may become such a daunting, distant, and unattainable achievement that, as a motivational goal, it would not have any great or lasting value since the aspiration it embraces is too great, as well as too distant. Rather, the immediate emphasis and concentration must be to focus on the *match* about to be played - *and the winning of that.* That then becomes the first stepping stone, the first sub-goal, and its achievement will provide the motivation to tackle the next goal - *to win the next match in round two.* And so on, and so on - keeping speculation and worry over the final win until the player is *actually confronted with the final contest.* By then he or she will be at a peak of excitement and potential achievement, having reached that pitch through the attainment of a series of realised sub-goals - each in itself an important step on the motivational journey.

The whole point is that things get done *by doing them,* not *by thinking or talking about them!*

Opportunities are grabbed by the *now* people whilst the *if/when* people are still fussing over how they will manage the challenge - *rather than asking themselves **why** they should accept it.*

> *'...all good things come to those who wait...*
> *...but only what is left behind by those who seize opportunities!'*
> - Abraham Lincoln

THE POWER OF THE SUBCONSCIOUS

I have already mentioned the fascinating phenomenon known as 'group dynamics'. Since we have been discussing *attitude*, it is interesting to note that there is a curious example of *collective attitude* - a sort of group dynamic - that emerges on a regular basis several times a year in Britain, notably at Christmas, Easter and at the approach of all Bank Holidays. These occasions create a sort of occupational constipation, a national obstruction to endeavour which may appear up to a week before each festival. It is as though a barricade had been erected which we can clearly see is barring the road ahead. The collective subconscious is not slow to get wind of these situations, and reacts by providing all the comparative, historic data to encourage the idea that there is little point in doing anything until *'after the holiday'*. The implication of this is an extravagantly wanton waste of man-hours as the working population, lemming-like, rushes towards complete national lethargy.

There is a story told of a young man joining the sales organisation of a financial services company a fortnight before Christmas. In his first two weeks he produced amazing sales figures, outstripping colleagues who had been with the organisation for years. His manager, fascinated by this performance, asked him how he managed it, in a period when sales are known to slump because people do not buy financial services contracts in the two week period preceding Christmas. The young man answered simply '...nobody told *me* that!'

Millions of working hours must be lost every year in this grey zone that precedes our national holidays, not to mention the hangover of even more wasted time that is so often the conclusion of this sorry pattern.

THE POWER OF THE SUBCONSCIOUS

Extremes of weather - for which Britain is famous - bring out the same symptoms of national group time-wasting. We all love a good crisis, for that is what breaks down national reserve and creates the fertile ground for an orgy of crisis bonding, rarely seen since the end of the last war. We adore the situations which allow us to behave towards one another in ways that are normally quite unacceptable. The weather crisis brings everything to a halt - but not entirely as a result of natural causes. The collective subconscious plays its part stoically, producing a broadsheet of notions that convinces us that there is little point in trying to get to work, in the happy anticipation of worsening conditions. Paradoxically, part of the ritual demands that intrepid journeys must be made. These come under the special heading of *'getting through'*, allowing us to indulge in an enjoyable excess of panic food buying, the natural preparation for (hopefully) a prolonged, enforced stay-at-home. Everyone wallows in a plethora of community misfortune when pipes freeze, snow drifts pile up and have to be moved, and crisis tea making achieves epidemic proportions. The whole nation is now in an over-drive of group time-wasting. And the blame for all this bizarre behaviour must be attributed to the collective subconscious, through its innocent functions of motivationally fuelling the fires with the stimulating feedback it constantly provides.

All our thinking is composed of negatives and positives. The subconscious is content with either mode of operation as it will embrace either totally, with equal enthusiasm. As we have seen, the subconscious is not a reasoning machine. It acts on every instruction that is passed to it, and does it with breath-taking speed. It employs a filing system of staggering proportions and virtually unlimited capacity.

THE POWER OF THE SUBCONSCIOUS

It is said that we only use about 5% of our total inherited potential as human beings. Einstein declared that the average man uses no more than .02% of his intellectual capacity. Despite this, almost every word we have ever uttered, the sounds we have heard, a catalogue of smells and tastes we have experienced and everything we have ever seen or touched are all recorded, and most are instantly accessible. A few insignificant items will get lost along the way, maybe the result of dying brain cells. To say we have forgotten something, generally is not strictly accurate. It is probably that we are having a little temporary difficulty with the recall mechanism. The information is there - it's just winkling it out that presents the problem! The process, or mechanism of thinking, therefore, is a two-way traffic between our information gathering senses - seeing, feeling, hearing tasting, smelling - and our subconscious, which is constantly recording, evaluating, comparing, and providing the feed-back we need to guide our decision-making. The brain with its virtually unlimited storage capacity, divides its function between long and short term storage. People often marvel at the fact that they can remember things from years ago, yet have difficulty in recalling what they did yesterday. This, I think, is because the short term storage facility is really nothing more than a pad on which notes may be scribbled and obliterated at will - rather like those 'magic' drawing slates we had as children. What is of real value is upgraded and moved across to be stored in the long term memory bank, whilst the merely trivial is erased and forgotten. Like a computer, we all have the *save & continue* facility to ensure that nothing of value is lost.

A computer is a restless creature. As long as it is switched on, even though it is not actually being used, it is constantly

THE POWER OF THE SUBCONSCIOUS

checking and re-checking for anything it should be doing, anxious to be ready instantly to respond to the next command. In exactly the same way, the subconscious, even while we sleep, never actually ceases its activity. It is always ready to respond to any crumb of input that may be offered. It may at times appear to be a little confused - and this, I suspect, might be the stuff of which dreams are composed.

The extraordinary images we experience in sleep happen, I believe, because the subconscious *is* always on duty and never actually shuts down. The thinking, experiencing, every-day side of the mechanism is at rest and therefore making little demand on the subconscious, nor is it presenting it with anything much in the way of new material on which to get to work. Odd, erratic thoughts and half-formed ideas flit through the system and the subconscious picks up on every one, providing, so far as it is possible, the usual flow and return of comparative information. It is as though a filing clerk is frenziedly rushing around, pulling information from the system in a haphazard and random manner, and presenting it for our inspection - not unlike a faithful dog retrieving a stick. Because of the haphazard inaccuracy of the stimuli, a lot of the resultant feed-back may well have the appearance of utter nonsense. The sleeping mind accepts these odd images, adds its own embroidery and presents the subconscious with a ludicrous package of even greater nonsense - the bizarre result is dreams and nightmares.

Painting is a process that links the two halves of the brain, the left-hand side, concerned with the rational and the practical, and the right-hand side, concerned more with intuition and creativity. Any creative painter will tell you that the act of

THE POWER OF THE SUBCONSCIOUS

making a painting is not unlike the holding of a conversation. He is faced initially with an intimidatingly blank canvas on which he must make some form of mark as a starting point - a commitment. This is like an opening statement which, conversationally, would require a response. The moment the painter makes this act of commitment, wherever the mark is placed, and whatever its form, the canvas says something back to him that will dictate what he should do next. His job is to watch, listen and respond (*awareness*) to what the painting is saying to him. He may of course disagree with what he sees developing. That is always his prerogative. He makes more marks on the canvas, and the process of discourse, statement and response starts again. The true act of creation is a matter of listening, watching and responding, using the subconscious as a creative tool to bridge the gap between practicality and intuition.

If in our daily lives we were to spend more time in being *aware*, listening to our subconscious, and responding to its invaluable output, the benefits could be quite startling. We must learn to *listen* - and to practice this skill, for that is what it is. It is not always easy because the messages can come thick and fast, usually presented with disarming simplicity and uncanny accuracy. If we are not truly listening, much of real value may pass us by. We need to cultivate an attitude of belief in the value of what our subconscious presents to us, and be prepared, through total trust, to act on the information we receive. We should aim to develop the courage of the partially sighted man who must - often for the sake of his own survival - react immediately to what he *thinks* he sees. If he hesitates or stops to analyse or question the hazy images that instinct has interpreted, he could, at worst, be placing himself at great personal risk.

THE POWER OF THE SUBCONSCIOUS

By listening to our inner voice, and acting on its instructions, we may hugely improve our general efficiency, thus making better and more decisive judgements, enhancing our relationships with others, experiencing the achievement of our goals and ambitions more easily, and discovering a greater fulfilment and enrichment in every aspect of our living.

The first step in this process is learning to control negative thoughts without allowing our subconscious the opportunity to demotivate us. It cannot do this of its own accord of course, for as we have seen, it has no actual intent, being merely a provider of the information necessary to the decision-making process.

We have already seen that there is a danger in associating with negative people, because their attitude, like boredom, is a destructive cancer which, given the right conditions in which to develop and flourish, will spread rapidly. Constantly talking about and dwelling on negative things actually has a potential for attracting more negatives into our lives. There are some people - and we have all met them - who seem to be constantly beset by problems. Nobody else has worries quite like theirs, indeed, they seem to enjoy a sort of love affair with problems, and show a total reluctance to let go of them. No matter how the conversational flow develops, they will always manage to turn attention back to themselves and their perpetual, imagined yet over-dramatised difficulties. Do try to avoid such people for they are death to those with higher aspirations. They have the ability to infect whole groups, dragging them down a spiral of demotivation, to plunge them collectively into a depression that few individuals could achieve on their own.

THE POWER OF THE SUBCONSCIOUS

In the course of our daily lives we all accumulate a great deal of both mental and physical rubbish with which we surround ourselves - that excess baggage I have already mentioned. This is yet another aspect of negativism. *Be bold! Eliminate everything from your life that makes no positive contribution to it!* There is the greatest satisfaction in throwing out this irrelevant accumulation of junk, without which we will be able to travel faster and more easily.

On a purely practical note, go through your wardrobe and discard everything you do not wear! We are all too good at persuading ourselves that *it might come in useful one day.* We know perfectly well that we are only postponing the inevitable time when we will throw the it away!

The point is that all the time we remain custodians of these extraneous millstones, we are unconsciously being drained of energy through the sheer weight of the responsibility. Why else should we feel such a sense of light-headed delight when we have cast off the burden?

Just as your car needs regular servicing, your body needs regular exercise - and so does your brain. It enjoys being stretched and stimulated, for this is what keeps it in peak condition.

It is perhaps surprising to learn that the brain uses language rather than visual imagery in its storage and recall functions. It is logical to suppose that, on the basis of this fact, the greater and more effective your grasp of language and its uses, the more lively and effective will be your mental processes. Just as your body requires physical stimulation to avoid becoming sluggish, your brain needs to be constantly stretched to avoid stagnation.

THE POWER OF THE SUBCONSCIOUS

Read regularly so as to push your brain and exercise your intellect. Read the sort of material that normally you might avoid as looking 'too difficult'. Not only will your vocabulary increase, but your actual use of language will be enhanced and enriched. Cross-word puzzles are an excellent form of mental exercise. And the result of all this stimulus? The depth and complexity of your thinking will increase in direct ratio to the quality of the language you use, and the breadth your vocabulary has attained.

The brain delights in and thrives on new experience, innovation, variety, and surprise, so deny it nothing in its quest for stimulation, novelty, fun, and exercise - this way you will never be demoralised or demotivated by boredom - in fact, there will be no room for such depressing indulgence, and you won't even know what boredom is!

Positive action:
Believe in the amazing powers that are locked inside you. They are yours to use and control.

Give your subconscious the chance to show you what it is capable of. Try its powers as a problem solver...

1. Write out your problem clearly and in detail.

2. Try to find a solution for yourself, as a first resort.

3. If you cannot see the answer, ask your subconscious to resolve the problem for you. Pose the question and its alternatives clearly and concisely. Set a time limit for receiving the answer - say, tomorrow morning or in 24 hours time.

THE POWER OF THE SUBCONSCIOUS

4. Here is the most important part of the exercise - *forget the problem completely.* There is no point in keeping a dog and barking yourself!

5. The answer is not going to be revealed to you in letters of fire. Be very *aware* of everything that passes through your mind. 'Listen' in the silence for hunches, flashes of inspiration, sudden thoughts. These will often provide pointers to the solution. The great thing is to believe strongly enough in what you are doing, and to be prepared to *act* on what is suggested to you.

Be a *now* person! Practise the strategy of immediate action in all things. Never put off anything until tomorrow that you could easily do today. Make your slogan - *do it now!*

Remember it is *you* who influences your subconscious - *never forget who is the master and who the servant!*

5
Seeking change

Each of us has always been - or so we like to think - the manager of our own affairs, the master of our own destiny. We persuade ourselves that we are able to make anything we wish of our lives . If this is so, hands up those who are truly satisfied with the end result! If we are so clever, how come we are so confused and disorganised?

In seeking change, the implication must surely be that we are not exactly in charge, not entirely satisfied with the status quo. Most of us tend to muddle through life fighting fires when and where they occur, rather than seriously planning (fire prevention!) to achieve positive results.

If we are to create permanent change and improvement, planning is the only positive way it can be achieved.

Change must always have its starting point, and that often calls for a general clear-out, discarding the physical rubbish of our lives to make way for the new. Not for nothing do we use that old chestnut...*'a new broom sweeps clean'* !

As we stand on our new launch platform we must decide on the precise nature of the change we desire for ourselves. What are our priorities? Success and real achievement would be high on most people's agenda, but true success in life is made up of so many elements, we really need to pin down just what it implies to each one of us as individuals. Performance skills, since these can be acquired through teaching, cannot be regarded as representing success in the truest sense. But if such skills could be developed whilst, at the same time, enriching and improving relationships with our fellow human beings, we might be getting closer to a significant meaning of success.

My belief is that true success lies in the attainment of enjoyment, related to a general expansion of self, an enrichment and development of all our talents and personal attributes. We must have a sincere desire not just to enrich our own lives but to bring greater quality to the lives of those whose lives we touch as we travel towards the achievement of our personal goals. A *total enjoyment,* expressed in everything we do - not merely the seeking after *pleasure* - seems to embody the real meaning of success.   Seeking after *pleasure* is a purely transitory thing. We may experience real pleasure from the enjoyment of a splendid meal, but once that meal is over, *that is that*! The experience can of course be repeated, and almost the same degree of pleasure recreated, but the experience is merely a thing of the moment.

Enjoyment is different. It is an experience of a deeper, broader and more permanently significant nature. We have the ability to lose ourselves in true enjoyment, whether it be in work, music, art, good company and conversation,   or anything else we may do.   This total emersion of oneself is the very nature of the force I have called *Dynamic Energy (DE).* It is the complete absorption of all one's energy and attention, concentrated and aimed at one specific thing, in one particular direction. This, surely, is getting closer to the essential ingredient of true success and achievement?   It embodies the full, unqualified enjoyment of life and all one may do in living it successfully.

Psychologists talk of a syndrome they know as *the law of cause and effect.*   It is concerned with *reciprocal action.* Most of us are more familiar with the words used in the Bible: *'...as ye sow, so shall ye reap'.*   What we get out of life will

SEEKING CHANGE

always be in direct ratio to the measure of what we put into it. That is recripocal action. The way in which things have turned out for any of us in life is merely a reflection of how good or bad a manager we have proved to be. It is neither just, honest, nor reasonable to apportion blame to any person or to circumstance outside ourselves. We call the shots, and we benefit or suffer from the consequences of our own actions. Once we give up blaming other people or outside circumstances for our own inadequacies, and begin to understand the nature of responsibility, we actually begin to enjoy a new freedom.

Human behaviour is sometimes represented as a spectrum or scale, one end of which represents total irresponsibility, the other, responsibility. The completely disturbed person would be located at the irresponsibility end, whilst total normality - whatever that means - is located at the other end. Responsibility, looked at in this way, takes on a whole new meaning - responsibility for our own actions as well as for the control of our mental processes, since all actions - other than the involuntary - originate through thought.

We all suffer negative thoughts and emotions and these will determine where we are placed on the responsibility scale, so, in reality, our position on that scale is in a constant state of change. These changes - the result of emotional swings - can often produce quite dramatic modes of behaviour.

Doubt, resentment, jealousy, guilt, envy - all are capable of undermining - even causing serious damage to - the rhythm of our lives and upsetting the balance of what we hope is the responsible human state. Every single day we are capable of reducing ourselves to the equivalent of temporary psychological cripples as we enact the motions of self-pity, anger, resentment and blame. We permit these unworthy emotions to enter our inner mental sanctum where they quickly grow and multiply, in precisely the same way a virus will on gaining entry to our bodies. Many negative emotional states can be traced to mere foolish imaginings - the presumptive notion that *we know what others are thinking.* Let's knock this notion on the head right now! - *there is no way we can gain access to the thoughts of others.*

We all have a way of writing our own scenario. Then our subconscious takes over the script, reacting to and embellishing it until we have produced a mental state that completely distorts our thinking. We go on, with the aid of our subconscious, producing a flood of inaccurate and fictitious information, often charged with very real emotion. Our behaviour then begins to reflect this distorted imagery and we begin to react in ways that confuse the issue still further! Most personal conflicts develop through this pattern.

Normally we would want to rid ourselves of these damaging elements, but all too often, out of either ignorance or stupidity, we go out of our way to justify them, adding further fuel to an already over-charged situation. But - and I feel sure you will realise this by now - it is our *subconscious* that is doing the stirring, because *we do have personal choice* so long as we make the deliberate effort to *regain control of our thought processes.*

There is a kind of self-poisoning in negative attitudes and behaviour, but because it emanates from a mental process, it can actually be controlled. The key to this control is to maintain a constant *awareness* of what is happening, coupled to the all-important realisation that...

'... *I am responsible*'

SEEKING CHANGE

Negative emotions are actually difficult to sustain for any length of time unless there is the opportunity to keep justifying our feelings by sharing them with other people. Do make the decision not to associate willingly with negative people. *Do not* become the person who demotivates others! Aim to develop an attitude of neutrality which does not recognise the idea of *knowing what others are thinking.* This is the only way to defeat the process that allows the subconscious to (innocently) generate that dangerous condition of negative energy which is so destructive and spiritually undermining.

There is an interesting experiment that anyone can try - and the outcome will be surprisingly beneficial. Make a declaration between yourself and your partner - or a friend - that neither will criticise the other for a period of 10 days! If either party breaks the pact, the 10 days starts again. After a few false starts, you will be surprised at the result!

All of us, as we have seen, have a habit of persuading ourselves that external circumstances are the cause of our own negative emotions. And we have now seen that this is not always the case - *confusing!* Negative emotions are the result of *our response* to outside agencies before the subconscious gets to work, justifying and developing the initial mental attitude. In this process, all that is actually taking place is that we are fanning the flames of a fictitious drama (entirely of our own devising) that is rapidly getting out of control - *and this situation has the power and the potential to consume us.* If we can manage to first recognise and then halt or reverse the process to give ourselves the opportunity to disengage from a scenario *which we have instigated,* we have the chance to regain control of our emotional machinery again

SEEKING CHANGE

- allowing us to turn our backs and walk away from our own folly, completely unscathed.

This represents the greatest conquest of self, and a great step forward in the process of change and self-development. It is the ultimate demonstration of the truth in the statement that...

> *...if we want our circumstances to change,
> it is we that must change first.*

6
Who is in charge?

Plato, the Athenian philosopher, said...
*'The first and best victory is to conquer self.
To be conquered by self, is of all things,
the most shameful and vile.'*

Obviously, in the quest for change and personal development, the taking of decisions is a matter of real importance. Remember, the subconscious is going to play a significant role in carrying out the requirements of any decisions you may make, so, with the knowledge you now have of the mechanism with which you are dealing, you cannot afford to be too woolly about how you express those decisions! They must be firm, decisive and precise. To take an example, if it was your intention to try and kick the smoking habit it would be no use at all saying to yourself *'...I think, if I really tried, I could probably stop smoking.'* Such a statement has *provisional failure* written all over it. It lacks *commitment*, has no time scale, and is devoid of any real conviction. With information as indefinite as that, your subconscious would have a heyday!

If, on the other hand you were to make the declaration *'I will stop smoking as of this moment!'* - there is nothing more to be said. The job is done, the commitment made, and the time scale set. It is simply not possible to partially stop smoking - you either smoke or you don't. The decision can only be total and final. *A decision with in-built possibilities is no decision at all.* The only built-in factor must be *commitment*.

WHO IS IN CHARGE?

A decision based on real commitment and total belief in its outcome has a way of causing events - making things happen. If you decide what you really desire, and force yourself to take any appropriate action, you are creating the necessary momentum to achieve a definite result. This is just part of the mechanism I have already touched on - *Dynamic Energy* - and one of the functions of *DE* is to produce the *'success-breeds-success'* syndrome.

The subconscious, through its constant evaluation and assessment function, is your in-built decision-making aid. Notice I did not say *'your decision-maker'*. The mechanism is, as I must keep emphasising, *yours* to control. But before that can happen, any previously imposed controls governing attitudinal and behavioural patterns that are detrimental to the decision making process must be removed. These would probably be controls and inhibitions imposed, possibly years earlier, by teachers and/or parents - with every well-meaning intention, it must be said - as well as the more insidious influences of television and advertising.

Too often these preconditioned influences are the cause of unconscious worries and confusion. They have a way of imposing unnecessary constraints and controls that anticipate future action even before any conscious decision has been made. The result can often be that we leave undone things that should have been dealt with, and that we feel an obligation to do certain things that we do not truly want to do. This mental world of ours is, without doubt, a battle field!

But, never forget, choice is always yours! It is for us to choose between allowing ourselves to go on being influenced by past conditioning, or to take control of the decision-making mechanism, and by so doing, ensure we have complete mastery over the possibilities of change.

WHO IS IN CHARGE?

Inevitably we will occasionally make poor decisions. This is of little account and certainly nothing to worry about. Never be afraid of making a bad decision. Learn to look on such occurrences as situations from which you may learn and develop. Life cannot only be composed of 'ups' - there will always be 'downs' too. After all, where did you come from to arrive at an 'up'? It is the 'downs' in life that make the 'ups' possible - and exciting. A hill is only a hill because it sits between two valleys - and vice versa. So, learn and profit from the poor decisions you may have made, for then it is unlikely you will ever make the same mistake again!

Looking at the very worst that life can hand you, if you have been knocked to the very bottom, *you still have choice!* - you have the choice to stay there wallowing in destructive self-pity, or you can make the conscious decision to do something about your situation, and get up. To make such a decision sometimes requires courage and determination of a high degree, but the commitment made will be the thing that can kick-start your life again, and begin the total recovery and revival process.

Making decisions is not the same thing as stating preferences. That is the difference between *expectation* and *wishing.* In making what we think is a positive decision, we often spend too much time worrying about *how* the desired end result can be achieved - and this may even affect the decision we eventually make. I have already touched on the difference between these two small words, *how* and *why,* but this point is of such fundamental importance, it is worth exploring a little further.

The first question to ask oneself when confronted with the need for a decision is *why?* Why does the decision have

WHO IS IN CHARGE?

to be made? Why is the outcome necessary? *Why* clarifies intent and pinpoints need. Once these things are clearly established in the mind, and the decision has been made, *how* the task is to be carried out will, from then on, be so much clearer - and the energy to carry the decision through will easily be generated. So the process is...

1. The decision is made (based on *expectation* and the *desire* for a result).
2. *Immediate* action (*commitment*).
3. A heightened *awareness* to recognise the answer to the *how* question when it reveals itself.

True decision taking requires both guts and courage. Any committed decision has a splendid finality about it that is its own ultimate guarantee of a successful conclusion.

Decisions of this sort leave feelings of real satisfaction in their wake and build an energy level that will create one success on the heels of another. This is *Dynamic Energy* working at full capacity.

Successful people are making vital, committed decisions all the time - decisions they are willing to stand by and on which they are prepared to stake their reputation. The job of the chairman of a large company is to make decisions that will affect the on-going success (or failure) of his company and could influence the lives of hundreds of other people. However, this same man may, on a personal level, find it extremely difficult to cope with a single decision that will affect nobody but himself. Supposing he is being pressurised to stop smoking. The decision-making process becomes complicated by one element that doesn't normally bother him in his working life - *personal choice* or *desire*. Does he really *want* to stop smoking? Does he have a real *desire* to

WHO IS IN CHARGE?

do so? He may be being nagged. He is probably well aware of the danger to his health - but, without the *desire* to stop there will be no *commitment*, and therefore nothing to trigger the necessary action needed to carry the project easily towards a defined goal.

Desire for change must precede commitment to action.

Decision-making is a skill, and, like all skills, can be acquired and will improve with practice. It is always easier to put off a decision than to make one. Many people drift through life happily allowing others to make decisions for them. This is the easy option - the result is a loss of initiative, loss of drive, even possibly a loss of self-esteem, thus allowing a flabby attitude to develop. Carried a step further, the same person becomes cunningly adept at allocating blame for his or her own failure or lack of drive to other people or to outside circumstances, thereby side-stepping any feelings of personal responsibility.

Self-esteem is vital to the well-being of every one of us. Self-esteem can be greatly enhanced through the satisfaction that comes from *accepting responsibility* and making our own life-changing decisions - and having the personal dedication to carry them through to the achievement of significant goals.

It is easy to become lazy about decision-making. We can revert too readily to *wishing,* rather than making the effort that committed decisions require. Clearly, if this state of inertia is to be overcome, real change must take place.

Decision-making is the key to taking control of your life.

WHO IS IN CHARGE?

A decision is only worthwhile when it results in action - for it is action that brings about the change necessary to defeat inertia - the greatest single stumbling block to self-improvement and personal advancement. Inertia is often an amalgam of boredom and self-pity. It is the stagnating enemy that lurks within each one of us, watching and waiting for the opportunity to drag us down into a state of sluggish idleness.

One definition of inertia is *sloth* - and surely that is one of the seven deadly sins! So how do we combat the deadly potential of this sleazy and negative adversary? Massive action is the only answer! Massive action that results in massive activity. Taking control. Becoming a decision maker and taker, accepting responsibility for oneself and one's life.

When things are not going the way we wish, we can always make a choice and select our response. We might become angry and petulant, looking for someone or something to blame, or we could remain calm, reasonable and responsible, in the full understanding that we are in control.

When faced with the pressures of life, there is a very powerful thought that we can present to our subconscious, a thought that has the ability to defeat negative influences and emotions...

I am responsible!

Try repeating this several times - even aloud, if possible. You will be surprised at the result! It is actually difficult, whilst repeating this simple phrase to hang on to negative thoughts and feelings. It permits one to see where things may have gone wrong. It is a very revealing weapon.

WHO IS IN CHARGE?

I am responsible!

You will soon discover that this can be the key to ridding yourself of so much that simply is not worth holding on to. You must be the captain of your own destiny, the vessel for which you are totally responsible and of which you are totally in command.

The outcome of the 1992 General Election in Britain saw the Labour Party blaming both the Conservatives and the news media for their defeat. They appeared to be quite unaware that the responsibility for this lay with themselves. Either they failed to present themselves to the electorate as a sufficiently attractive alternative to Conservative government, or they were unwilling to face up to the possibility that the country did not, at that time, want a socialist government. Whichever way one looks at it, they were, totally responsible for their own down-fall. They made too many assumptions and failed to accept responsibility, resorting to attributing blame to others, and through that, added nothing to their party image.

Their fortunes only began to change when they recognised what had gone wrong, and made a determined effort to create change by assuming the public mantle of responsibility and presenting themselves as a credible proposition. And look what happened in May 1997!

If there is just one thing you remember after reading this book, I sincerely hope it is that simple but emotively loaded phrase...*I am responsible!*

Once you realise that blame for your own circumstances cannot be discarded, transferred, off-loaded or reallocated, and that external circumstances - other than, of course, the

WHO IS IN CHARGE?

purely physical - cannot touch or harm you, because they are only the products of your own imagined interpretation of things, *you are truly in charge.* You are indeed *responsible!*

The words *I believe,* have been described as the most emotive words in the English language. *Belief* is another vital component of success. There are many attributes necessary, as we have seen, not least intelligence and ability, but belief in yourself and in your ability to achieve is the one single ingredient that can carry you to the most exciting areas of life. It has the power and ability to demolish barriers, break down restrictions and inhibitions and allow one to travel just as far as one wishes to go. With belief all things are possible, all goals achievable.

Belief comes in several forms...

- Belief in one's self, and in one's ideals.
- Belief in what one is doing - and in one's ability to do it.
- Belief in others, and in their abilities.
- Belief in the strength of one's own thoughts.
- Belief in the goals one sets, and belief in the possibility of their achievement.

Sports men and women understand belief and are excellent examples of the effects of belief in action. At the highest levels, in sport of all kinds, where events are won or lost on the basis of fractions of a second, mental preparation is of supreme importance. The subconscious must be totally under control - totally *convinced* that there is no possible or conceivable alternative to winning. Not even the minutest doubt can be allowed to creep in.

WHO IS IN CHARGE?

The competitor's performance is rehearsed over and over in the mind so that the whole winning scenario is firmly embedded within the subconscious. This is a matter of total *focus* on a very specifically defined goal, and it represents belief of the very highest order.

There are many games that are played in the mind - golf, snooker and tennis are three good examples. As a spectator, it is fascinating to watch the domination of the game swinging back and forth between the competitors as psychological advantages boost or demoralise each player in turn. When one player is on top, one can clearly see *Dynamic Energy* swinging into action, boosting performance and making all things possible. Supremely positive attitudes embodying certainty and expectation have taken control as the other competitor is dominated by this surge of inner energy. He will begin to demonstrate all the signs of demotivation, developing the potential for making minor mistakes, as a temporary loss of focus, so necessary to the winning attitude, slips away.

Under these circumstances the subconscious can easily become the enemy in its innocent search for feed back from previous experience. Until a mental adjustment can be made and the subconscious is mastered and put under control again, to provide images of success and achievement - it will go on compiling evidence from past experience, such as defeat on previous occasions. The sports man or woman must always hold on to the mental images of his or her greatest triumphs, and especially to the *feelings that accompanied those precious occasions.*

It is possible for a world class athlete to develop a mental attitude which ensures that the really big prizes always elude him or her, leaving the residual image of always having to accept second place. When real victory is almost in the

WHO IS IN CHARGE?

contestant's grasp, the subconscious has a nasty way of replaying past experience - certain death to the idea of now becoming the victor. This mould can be very difficult to break. Only the strongest mental attitudes have any chance of overcoming the situation. It is essential to develop the *certain belief* that accepting second place is a thing of the past. No 'ifs' or 'buts' - that has got to be established as a positive fact! Mental images, as we have seen, must be generated to persuade the athlete to reconstruct the feelings he had when winning a major event, and then hold this image firmly in the forefront of his mind.

The athlete, whatever the sport, has to be totally in control of his emotions and to be sure that the *desire* to win is so strongly established, that it is impossible for any grain of doubt to survive. Only the winning position will do - and this concept must be strongly embedded when victory is in sight, completely obscuring and obliterating all past emotions. Instead of presenting that depressing second-place-syndrome, the subconscious produces inspiration in the form of a massive surge of extra positive energy carrying the contestant to victory. This action will certainly be transmitted to opponents who, under the sudden extra pressure, are liable to crumble and start making the mistakes that will very likely lose the contest.

In a world-class tennis match, the psychological advantage swings back and forth between the players as they battle for motivational supremacy, not just through the use of brilliant technical and athletic skills, but just as much through the mental attitudes they are able to bring to the game. Each player senses who is on top, and who is the under dog.

Some players can become so intensely focused that, providing nothing disturbs it, their opponent is dominated psychologically, and is quickly pushed to that point where mistakes begin to be made.

Human beings respond gloriously to their own effort. The greater the effort - and through that, the resultant generated energy - the more their interest is stimulated. They stop making excuses for their situation and begin to realise the value of conditions such as freedom, happiness, enthusiasm, joy, and the excitement of real commitment. Interest and the full enjoyment of what one is doing produces its own kind of energy, but it is *effort* that fires it, and hey presto! - we have created that *'moving or impelling power'*. This is the process of *Dynamic Energy*.

The word *dynamic* clearly has the same roots as *dynamo*. A dynamo is involved with two forms of energy. It requires energy of one kind to start it up and to keep it running, then, whilst it *is* running, it is, itself, generating an abundant supply of electrical energy. Perhaps, from here on, we should abbreviate the expression *Dynamic Energy* to *DE* - a phenomenon well worth exploring further...

Positive action:

1. Repeat to yourself - *aloud* - at least 10 times a day:
   I am responsible! Remember it whenever
   there is a tendency to blame others, or to blame
   circumstances for something that you feel is not right.

2. Try to set at least two goals each day. Nothing too
   dramatic! They may only be small things, but in
   the achievement of them, you will have been lead
   into positive action of one sort or another.

WHO IS IN CHARGE?

3. Cultivate the habit of asking the question *'WHY'*,
   rather than *'HOW'* when faced with a problem,
   or the need to make an important decision.
   The *WHY* route will usually provide the answers
   you are seeking.
   The *HOW* route too often leads down a cul-de-sac.

7
Dynamic Energy - DE

It has often been pointed out by psychologists that money is not, as many suppose, the great motivator. It must be admitted though, that having no money at all does tend to concentrate the mind, introducing a definite motivational aspect into the equation. But to those who have even modest earnings, it is *recognition* that is the real motivator - the fundamental human need *to be seen to have succeeded.*

Similarly, the acquisition of wealth and worldly goods cannot be regarded as a universal formula for happiness. The trouble with being rich is that acquisition tends to promote feelings of disillusionment. People can very quickly get used to having money and tend, as a result, to want more and more. What they perceive as the ultimate goal of happiness is always just out of reach - and what might have been happiness is replaced by vague feelings of discontent, and worries that something may go wrong. This condition has been aptly christened *The Paradise Syndrome.*

But *happiness,* as we have already seen, is only a transitory, *now* experience. It is the gratification of some immediate wish or desire which, once enjoyed, can be put back on the shelf until the next time we wish to enjoy the same or a similar experience again.

To experience a truly fulfilled life we need to seek *enjoyment* - and that means *enjoyment in everything we do.* To enjoy life is to live life to the full. Human beings function at their very best when they are fully occupied and in pursuit of meaningful goals that they have clearly and precisely

DYNAMIC ENERGY - *DE*

defined and planned for themselves. The achievement of a substantial goal may involve the achievement of several lesser goals - stepping stones towards the main event. The provision of a continuous chain reaction of small accomplishments, points of satisfaction along the way, a sort of drip-feed of stimulants, will keep one's eye on the main target. But, once that target has been achieved, it must be quickly replaced by another, possibly more stretching goal.

When we are totally absorbed in the challenge of a goal, *DE* is operating at full throttle. *DE* is the flowing force that takes hold of us when we are completely focused, totally submerged in any activity, be it wood carving, creative cooking, sex, writing, painting, driving a powerful car, climbing a difficult rock face - in fact any activity that has the ability to engage our absolute concentration. The result can be a kind of isolated oblivion equating to complete enjoyment - to the extent that we become unaware of both time and surroundings. Time itself can be changed by such experiences. It will adapt to suit *us,* freeing us from the bondage it so often imposes.

I have already mentioned the process involved in the production of a truly creative painting - the 'dialogue' that develops between the painter and his canvas. This very same process is the basis of every activity that can carry one into the state of *DE,* because, to flourish and develop and sustain itself, *DE* requires a constant flow of feed-back. There must be a two-way stream of vital information, allowing us to see just how our task is developing, whilst advancing towards the natural goal or achievement.

The establishing, accepting, and achieving of goals is a matter of supreme enjoyment to us, for without them we have

DYNAMIC ENERGY - *DE*

a tendency to flounder and slip into a state of fairly meaningless existence. We have a fundamental need for new challenges and constant stimulation, and the feed-back from such experience keeps us in touch, moment by moment, so that we always know just what we have to do. It has been observed by scientists that animals kept in a state of permanent activity are the ones that live the longest. This equates totally with the human condition. Think of the most lively, dynamic old people you know. They are certainly not couch potatoes! They are people who have kept their minds fully alive by constant stimulation and interest, and, within certain obvious parameters, even the body has responded too, so far as physical defects will allow. Such people usually remain mentally active long after the physical machine has run itself into the ground.

The very fact of planning every moment and every move, keeps us in a state of personal *awareness*, and *awareness* makes for greater enjoyment - the state we should always seek to achieve. Challenges are important, but these must be matched to capability. A task which is too difficult simply produces stress. Conversely, if the task is too simple, the result can be boredom. Either outcome adds nothing to our overall search for true enjoyment.

We should always strive towards an awareness of the present - where we are *now*, what we are doing - *now*. If we can free ourselves from the past and even from the future, we have a real chance of achieving true *focus*, and that equates to the thing we have been talking about so much - *awareness*. This can be a completely new and exciting experience, for it is taking control of our own life in a way that we may never have done before.

DYNAMIC ENERGY - *DE*

Enjoyment can be found in all things - in work, play, social obligations. In our upbringing, particularly under the influence of parents, we may easily have come to see 'work' as an unpleasant but necessary chore, and 'play' as definitely pleasant, if possibly a touch trivial. This is because a serious importance was, at some time, placed on the concept of *work*, whilst *play* was surrounded by feelings of frivolity.

As we approached adulthood, we came to know work or occupation as the situation in which the real challenges of life were to be met, a place where goals were both clear and precise. In our non-working hours, there were few goals, giving our free time a certain sense of emptiness, even bordering on worthlessness. Psychologically the unconscious tendency is to feel happier and more contented at work (because we are more directionally satisfied) than when we are home, virtually doing nothing of any real significance. This is the psychological background that creates the workaholic who finds greater *quality* in constant, directional activity than in undirected idleness with which he finds it very difficult to cope. In essence, he experiences the joys of *DE* whilst at work, yet rarely finds true and satisfying enjoyment in relaxation and play.

But activity, simply for its own sake, is certainly not going to produce satisfaction. For example, a purely repetitive job on a production line lacks the necessary sense of focus required to produce a state of heightened enjoyment, simply because activity of this sort offers no defined goals. If a repetitive job happens to be your lot in life, it is important to try to bring variety to the tasks as a deviation or shield from the sheer boredom the job may induce. It may not actually be possible to change the world around you, but it *is* possible to change *your view of that world* so as to introduce a new perspective that might make the repetitive tasks more

DYNAMIC ENERGY - *DE*

acceptable. Create challenges for yourself, try to perceive the job in some new light so as to get more enjoyment from it. And that, of course, brings us back to the same concept we have already discussed in some detail - the idea that if you want your circumstances to change, it is *you* who must change first!

People have a *need* to enjoy their work, otherwise they are unlikely to reach their full potential. A happy workforce is a productive workforce. The employer who sees the sense in introducing some form of reward system - either based on individual incentive, or something devised on a more collective basis, will reap his own rewards. This is merely exploiting the concept that people need to have goals, for both commercial gain and individual satisfaction. The employees begin to enjoy their work more - and it is the people that are seen to be enjoying their work that tend to get noticed by their employers. These are the individuals most likely to be marked down for eventual promotion. So everybody wins! The more *enjoyment* that can be generated in the general working environment, the more likely it is that *DE* will start to operate and bring its own brand of magic and reward into an otherwise dull situation.

So success lies in *activity*, for when a person is active, that person is *focused* - they have direction and a real sense of purpose. They have *goals*. These are all fundamental ingredients of *enjoyment* - the trigger to all the magic of *DE*.

Remember - when DE is operating, all things are possible!

8
Peaks and troughs

We have all experienced depression at some time in our lives. The effect, to say the least, is distinctly demotivating! We enter a downward spiral which has the ability, if left unchecked, to carry us lower and lower until a point is reached at which our situation becomes very difficult to reverse. When this is happening we become our own worst enemy, for we are capable of quickly developing a tendency to fantasise and dramatise the down-side of any gloomy situation, caught up as we are, in a lemming-like rush towards the cliff edge of self-imposed emotional destruction.

Depression has the effect of forcing us to turn inwards, allowing emotions such as self-pity, remorse, dissatisfaction, feelings of injustice - indeed, the entire gamut of destructive negative experience, to get the upper hand. All this is achieved with the unasked for, and indeed unwanted, help of our subconscious! But, as we know only too well, it is only doing its job of providing comparative and immediate feed-back with its accustomed efficiency, in total ignorance of the outcome its actions can create. It is merely acting on statements made - in this case, the messages of depression - digging out all the evidence from the files to compound the situation. This action has the affect of creating unhappiness and promoting feelings of insecurity, which in turn causes the subconscious to go on perpetuating the downward spiral.

Once one has reached a really profound motivational low, it is difficult, though not by any means totally impossible, to climb back onto a relatively safe and positive

PEAKS AND TROUGHS

plateau. But it is important to think seriously about your situation and make the attempt to set yourself a goal or two to create a new directional pointer. Positive action must surely follow.

The only way to defeat the subconscious when it is operating in negative mode is to feed in very positive thoughts, and by so doing, set it the task of rebuilding your ego - vitally important to your swift recovery. As we know, the subconscious mechanism works just as well in either direction.

I make no pretence about this, it is certainly not easy to do these things when one is feeling spiritually shattered, but it is so important that the effort is made to force issues, for this is the *only* way to cope with a situation of this nature. Human beings tend to behave like a rudderless ship - that is *unless they have goals.*

When one is in a deeply demotivated state, the effort of a sudden burst of activity is like letting in the clutch whilst push-starting a car! The sheer drama of making that supreme and sudden effort will produce the surge of energy necessary to provide the vital spark needed to get the machine moving again!

A successful salesman will tell you that during his working week he becomes progressively more motivated through the successes his own sustained effort and activity have created. By Friday, as a result of this dynamic chain reaction, he is so highly charged that he almost resents the arrival of the weekend because it will bring an end to his relentless and ever-mounting state of excitement! But without the weekend, acting as a natural safety valve to release this urgent head of steam, he would probably self-destruct!

PEAKS AND TROUGHS

Fortunately, it is not possible to maintain such a high level of motivational excitement for any length of time. Motivational peaks certainly have value, but one must realise that peaks are only points of transience, they are not places of residence! The level of motivation required to attain a peak cannot be sustained for very long. If we were always at the zenith of achievement, there would come a point when it did not appear to be achievement any more. The sensation would become blunted, simply reducing the experience to the level of the commonplace. There would be no ups and downs, no peaks or troughs.

Achievement is a relative thing. How would we know we had reached a peak unless we had experienced the trough that preceded it? It is this contrast that makes our journey so worthwhile - how true it is that to travel hopefully is often better than to arrive! Hope, expectation and optimism are the most sustaining of human emotions. Without these elements, life would be a truly boring and drab affair. People who claim boredom as their special preserve, living without the sustaining values of emotions such as hope, expectation and optimism, are the real non-achievers in life, and deserve all that life brings them.

Motivational peaks and troughs are especially important to imaginative and creative people, providing the current that sets and keeps *DE* flowing. But beware, for there are odd occasions when the sheer generated energy of a situation can actually cause problems. Take the pop singer as an example of just what can happen. During a live gig the performer rises through all the levels of excitement at great speed, drawing energy and stimulation from the feedback the audience provides. The performer in turn stimulates the audience still further. *DE* is, at this stage, affecting everyone on a collective basis - *group dynamics* comes into play, producing an energy, surpassing in its powerful momentum, the combined input of every member of the audience. The performance eventually comes to an end and the pool of collective energy slowly dissipates as the audience breaks up and each individual carries away his small portion of this total, shared and unique experience. The performer, however, is left high and dry with the adrenalin still thundering through his system, but with nothing at which to direct or expend it. His mood slowly changes, modified by these altered circumstances. In purely practical terms this is no more than a chemical adjustment being made within the bodily system, but denied the stimulation that the audience had provided, the performer is left stranded like a beached whale, to face the difficult and often lonely descent from his artificial 'high'. It is not at all difficult to understand how tempting drugs might appear under such circumstances, offering a return to the peak of exciting feelings from which he has so suddenly withdrawn - an experience that cost a great deal in sheer physical energy to attain.

The feelings induced by drugs can in no way even begin to imitate the experience of *DE*. *DE* will motivate one into great creative activity, and through that be highly beneficial. Drugs may produce an uncontrolled transitory high that will inevitably be followed by a dramatic low - a situation of little benefit to anyone.

9
Goals, targets & recognition

As we are by now well aware, it is possible to motivate oneself through self-generated activity and to benefit from the stimulating cycle that is its natural and inevitable follow-on (*DE*). But, to produce real peaks of motivational excitement we need a target or goal - something at which to aim, a point in time which, when eventually reached, will represent a measurable achievement. Arrival is not always the most exciting or satisfying of events - sometimes it can even turn out to be something of a disappointing anti-climax - but the important thing is that *a point of arrival provides the reason and stimulus for having made the journey.*

Goals and targets play very necessary role in the motivational process. Achievement is a great stimulus in itself, but reward is just as important as it offers real confirmation of the achievement as well as providing that most important of all human needs - *recognition.*

If you were to question the majority of people about what they feel is the greatest human motivator, their answer would probably be...*Money!* - but, as we have already seen, they would be wrong! Money *is,* certainly, a strong motivational factor to the person who has none, but assuming we are discussing someone who has reasonable earnings - what would be the motivational trigger to really get him into action? Almost certainly it would be *recognition.* It is being seen, especially by his peers, to be successful. Obviously earning money *can* be motivational, for there will always be the urge to hit new heights - but it is *being seen* to earn a large

GOALS, TARGETS & RECOGNITION

amount, rather than the actual sum involved, that gives most individuals the greatest - and most gratifying - satisfaction.

Recognition is the enduring motivator in a competitive environment where winning is - often mistakenly - seen to be the only measure of real achievement. There is little that can equal the value of *being seen to succeed.*

Whilst on the subject of reward and recognition, let's take a brief look at management, for it is in this field that these factors have a particular prominence. Within a large company one of the most common mistakes made at all levels is to assume that a good performer no longer has any need for praise or stimulation. There is *never* a point at which it is no longer necessary, nor needed. Reward and recognition are important at *all* levels of development, regardless of how successful an employee may be. If good motivational support has been the norm for an employee whilst climbing the career ladder, and it is suddenly withdrawn, the employee will not only feel let down, he is likely to also begin to question his value - and this could be very damaging to his self-esteem, with the possibility of long-term repercussions.

Management at all levels should understand the importance of, and the need for, constant recognition of the efforts of all employees. The most dangerous assumption - *and yet this is a mistake that is constantly repeated* - is to expect an employee to slog on indefinitely, contentedly performing his or her tasks with ability and dedication. This unthinking silence on the part of management is probably rooted in feelings of complete satisfaction with the performance of the employee. But without some sort of 'pat on the head' as a demonstration of recognition and appreciation of the effort that has been made, how can the employee possibly know how his efforts are

GOALS, TARGETS & RECOGNITION

seen? Without such simple acts of recognition, the employee may begin to harbour doubts - doubts that will inevitably start to multiply, fired by imagination and encouraged by the workings of the subconscious - until an attitude of disappointment and disillusion develops, which will probably result in a measurable drop in efficiency.

There are occasions where disregard of the need for recognition is quite deliberate on the part of a manager, should he see the employee, through his or her efficiency, as posing a threat to his own position. Under such threatening circumstances the manager is not likely to do anything to encourage such a person. The next level of management, if on its toes, should quickly recognise what is happening and do something to rectify the matter - but here, possibly, the problem simply goes on repeating itself.

The painter, the writer, the inventor, in fact anyone who produces anything that relies on the recognition of others for its success, *must have feed-back* - it is their very life-blood. Without it they can, like a plant deprived of nourishment, metaphorically whither and die. All creative people have a fundamental need for an audience of some sort, for without the feed-back they get from others they often have little idea of the measure or worth of their own work. Recognition from others sets the scale, and may even become the catalyst that keeps on driving the creative process forward.

The recognition the creative person gets may be in the form of critical appraisal, or simply, and more practically, through the sale of their work. After all, sales certainly imply that a degree of recognition and empathy has been achieved, sufficient at least for one person to wish to acquire the work of another. Feed-back is elemental to the creative

GOALS, TARGETS & RECOGNITION

process, it keeps the creative fire burning, for no fire can stay alive indefinitely without fuel.

Recognition, then, is a most powerful motivator. In their desire to see their children succeed, parents - and teachers - often misunderstand the important role that recognition plays. Children in particular thrive on having their achievements noticed and commented upon. There is an understandable wish for well-meaning parents to see their children shine, but sometimes, intending to be helpful, yet not realising the destructive effect their action might have, they are too critical, when all the child is longing for is a kindly pat on the head. All the well-meaning parent needs to realise - and guard against - is the fact that, at worst, the over-critical parent can stifle talent.

Sometimes in adult life we experience vague feelings of inadequacy, and this can often be attributed to a lack of the right sort of parental understanding of fundamental needs in childhood.

Most of us remember school reports only too well! We very likely also recall the feelings we had as children when our parents read them. *'Could do better!'* What a devastatingly unimaginative remark that was - and probably still is. The child to whom that gem was applied may have been, in their own way, making a supreme effort, and all they needed to stimulate them further was a bit of praise and recognition to encourage even greater efforts. The comment *'could do better'* is the saddest put-down. Rather than being an encouraging remark intended to reveal potential, it implies that little effort has been made.

All things are relative, and the school report should reflect this, assuming there is a genuine intention on the part

GOALS, TARGETS & RECOGNITION

of the school, and indeed the teacher, to be of help and guidance to both parents and children.

Quite possibly the child *could* have done better, but simply telling it that will achieve remarkably little. Far better that the teacher had recognised that the child *had* achieved certain goals, no matter how trivial these may have been. There would then have been something really positive on which to build, and the child would have derived both pride and satisfaction from that small recognition. The parents would have reacted in a more positive way and provided the child with a much needed and helpful boost. Everyone would have benefited! The self-esteem of the child would have remained intact, and may even have been strengthened. New goals could then have been set, to provide new levels of achievement - all relevant to the ability of the child - at which to aim. These would have been both stimulating and motivational. How easy it is to record *'could do better'*...where the judgement is made by placing the child on a scale of general achievement - with scant regard for personal qualities and attributes - when the top of this scale represents *winners*, whilst the bottom, by definition, presumably represent *losers*. The positions on this scale are determined by exams and tests, often artificial situations to which some children respond much better than others. Ability cannot easily be measured and classified by a snap decision It is, rather, something demonstrated by the continuing scenario, and the good teacher will always recognise this.

The ability to learn is made so much easier when any form of *stress* can be removed from the learning process. Stress, today's much over-used buzz word, the value of which has become eroded by applying it too readily to situations which really do not warrant it.

In the USA amazing results have been achieved by a particularly innovative languages teacher whose philosophy is based on creating a completely relaxed and easy environment, where emphasis is placed on the students *not making any attempt to deliberately remember what they are being taught.* Within this system there are no tests, no exams, and no home work. Ideally there must be no feeling of the formal classroom, but rather, a relaxed and comfortable environment into which the pupils slide effortlessly, allowing for a completely natural receptivity. This method of teaching a language, based largely, as it is, on the removal of *stress*, coupled to a very specific method of presentation, has enabled pupils of quite modest standards to acquire a good and accurate working knowledge of a language *within one week*. Compare this to conventional study lasting for a number of years, employing normal teaching methods, at the end of which, there is no guarantee of success.

All of us have inherited emotions from our upbringing and some of these, not surprisingly, follow us into adulthood, often creating a sense of unease and vague apprehension, for which, at the time, we can see no reason. Such situations may occur when we are confronted by specific tasks or events. The resultant feelings are almost certainly rooted in repressed emotions bequeathed to us by parents or teachers, innocently unaware of the long-term effects their reprimands may have.

Being told as a child that *'you never seem to be able to do anything right'*, or confronted with questions such as *'why are you always so clumsy?'* or *'why don't you ever learn'* - all left their small scars, as these events became deeply embedded

GOALS, TARGETS & RECOGNITION

in the subconscious. Everything was tucked away, seemingly 'forgotten', buried deep in the filing system. Such feelings are what are known as *fear factors* and they have a habit, under certain circumstances in later life, of suddenly surfacing as strangely disturbing sensations. The result can be a vague and unaccountable feeling of inadequacy.

One of the purposes of this book is to create an awareness of feelings of this nature, thereby providing a means of 'dismantling' them, so they may be replaced by a more positive self-image. When we are aware of the origins of such emotions and fears, they become defused and are relatively easy to dismiss. Being able to remove these mental 'blocks' and make permanent behavioural adjustments will eventually allow you to become the sort of person you always felt you should have been. There is great personal satisfaction in realising that one has shed these foolishly inhibiting modes of behaviour. As with the exercise we did with unused clothing, this is a little bit more of life's excess baggage to be dumped by the wayside!

Children are born with very positive emotions - they cry when they are sad and laugh when they are happy. They are spontaneous and completely without inhibitions. Children learn by watching, but they can easily *develop* negative emotions and attitudes from the adults surrounding them - attitudes that may stay with them, if left unchecked, throughout life. Fortunately, when we attain adulthood, we do actually have the opportunity to do something to regain lost control.

Children also have a wonderful natural creative talent. They are blessed with an uncluttered, honest and uncomplicated view of the world about them. This is a gift granted to us all

GOALS, TARGETS & RECOGNITION

in equal measure. *But what happens to it?* As with so many things that surround him, man cannot resist interfering and meddling, always in the innocent belief that he can improve on the original. Parents and teachers, with every good intention, undermine and can destroy the child's natural gift by attempting to impose their ideas of order and 'rightness', under the mistaken premise that *'grown-ups know best'*. Maybe the time has come to get rid of the idea that age, by some miraculous process, bestows wisdom!

Children, left to their own devices, will produce the most marvellous, uninhibited drawings. *Every one of them can do this.* They have no hang-ups, no thoughts as to whether they are capable or not, *they just do it,* and in the main, the results are brilliant! They show an honest, clear, and uncluttered view of the world around them. Sadly, all but the cleverest teachers, cannot resist intervening. Bit by bit the *natural creativity is taught out of the child* as its view is suppressed, adjusted, modified, and forced into the mould of perceived adult correctness. My belief is that successful painters are simply those who have somehow, miraculously, managed to resist this 'teaching' process to retain their natural gift more or less intact.

Children are born fearless and brimful of a natural curiosity that leads them to explore and investigate everything they encounter. This is the true learning process. But again adults find it difficult to stand back and allow the child the freedom to learn his or her own way, even though sometimes the child may get hurt. But, surely, that is learning too? There are constant cries - usually born out of natural parental apprehension or fear - of *'leave that alone', 'don't touch', 'come down from there!'*. This constant but well-meaning bombardment serves merely to give the child the feeling that every time it steps outside certain boundaries, it gets punished - or at least, reprimanded. Echoes of this repetitive treatment can manifest itself in adult life as *fear of failure* - a conditioned reflex from the childhood pattern of authoritarian criticism. I don't imagine that anyone, employing these seemingly innocent reprimands, ever stops to consider what the cumulative effect might be on a child's developing sense of self-esteem - the value they place on their own perception of themselves.

Whenever possible, reward should go hand in hand with recognition, for this is the certain way of bestowing real value on achievement.

Reward can sometimes be a *contractual* arrangement - *'finish your home-work and you can have a sweet!'* That is reward directly related to a required action - little more than a bribe, in fact! This form of reward can, of course, produce a reverse effect - *the home-work may not get done unless the sweet is offered!*

In the world of the sales-oriented company, a good example of contractual reward is the Overseas Sales Convention - intended to be a veritable extravaganza, staged in some exotic venue at the employer's expense. But, as a potential reward, this can have a variety of effects...

> 1. To some the qualification is so far beyond their reach that they consider it unattainable, and make no effort. If this attitude goes unnoticed, the pattern can develop into progressive mediocrity, probably terminating in failure.

GOALS, TARGETS & RECOGNITION

2. To some the achievement of the qualification is inevitable, producing at best, a smug satisfaction and a blasé acceptance of the reward.

3. To those who *almost* made the qualification in the previous year, the reward has great motivational value. They are not going to allow such a near miss to happen again!

4. As the year of qualification progresses, those seen to be on course will certainly be stimulated to strive harder, especially as the dead-line draws near.

It is vitally important that the contractual reward, especially when the period of qualification is protracted, is of the highest quality and standard. Should the reward fall short of expectation or have the slightest hint of economy or cost-paring, *its value will be totally negated* - and the promoter will, in the eyes of his employees, be forever discredited.

So, as you can see, the contract reward, although perhaps a little artificial, has a definite place as a motivational device.

Within the context of this book, you can use the concept of contract reward for behavioural modification very effectively. Having set a goal for yourself, you might then contract yourself to receive some form of 'prize' or 'reward' - anything a bit out of the ordinary that you would really enjoy - but granted only after the goal is achieved! It will help considerably to actually write out the 'contract' as this acts as a

GOALS, TARGETS & RECOGNITION

means of reinforcement and endows the situation with greater importance.

Take, for example, the person trying to give up smoking. The contract could ideally have progressive rewards built into the programme in recognition of continuous achievement. It is most important that the reward falls into the 'treat' category so that it is truly appreciated - for that gives it maximum motivational value.

The contract can also be used as a blatant bribe, through denial - *no gin and tonic until you have cut the grass!* Or, to a child, *no television until you've finished your homework!*

To sum up, the greatest reward in terms of psychological satisfaction, comes through *recognition* - being *seen* to have achieved, and *having that achievement publicly recognised.*

The simple act of the head of a department walking up to an employee, and, in front of his peers, declaring what a fine job he has done, will always be of inestimable value to that employee - especially if the remark is accompanied by some form of physical contact - maybe nothing more than a hand laid casually on a shoulder. This physical contact, even though it is so slight, has tremendous value. The unconscious pleasure it can provoke goes right back to childhood programming - the strong need for touching, and particularly in the very early formative years, the affection signalled by physical contact. We really are strange creatures, are we not! But, having an understanding of some of these basic behavioural patterns can be of great value in helping us to modify and adjust unwanted inherited habits.

GOALS, TARGETS & RECOGNITION

Positive action:
1. If you are a parent, try to remember what it was like to be a child. Try not to frustrate your own children, and above all, try to avoid always wanting to *show* them *HOW!* Most of us - and that includes children - never mind being told *what* to do. What none of us likes *is being told how to do it!* This simply denies creativity and stifles initiative.

2. Always praise *publicly* and reprimand *privately*. Remember the value of *physical contact.*

3. Cultivate the habit of being more *outgoing.*

4. If you are a manager or an employer, develop the habit of constantly recognising the efforts of others. *Corporate loyalty* only becomes a reality when all levels of management become fully aware that recognition and reward are the most valuable tools in their possession.

10
False limitations...

We all like to think that we know ourselves well - but how many of us, I wonder, have grown up with a personal image of ourselves that is quite inaccurate? Should this be the case, we are in danger of being handicapped and limited perhaps, by a flawed and deluding self-image that we carry around as part of our everyday baggage. We may actually be obscuring our true potential, having convinced ourselves that our capabilities are distinctly limited. This personal view of ourselves - our self-image - may be very different to the way in which others perceive us and define our capabilities. But which picture is the more accurate...?

It is possible, because we may have developed a distorted view, that we have actually erected false barriers to personal achievement. If such self-indulgent ideas have really taken root and become a part of our persona, it is clearly important that we discard them as quickly as possible. This way, not only will we lighten our load still further, but by doing so, we will be able to travel faster and more easily.

I can almost hear your question - *easy to say that, but how do we set about doing it?* Obviously the first thing to do is to examine this self-image of ours and question whether the persona we have so carefully built up over the years is the *real* us. Is it *really* us? Does it represent the person we *feel* ourselves to be? Did we really intend to be quite like this? Remember, we do not have to accept anything simply because it is 'there'! As we have seen, circumstances and the influences of environment and upbringing may have produced

FALSE LIMITATIONS...

behavioural patterns that are actually obscuring our true personality.

When I first started using a sophisticated word processor, I was intrigued by its drawing function. But one thing fascinated me in particular, and that was a small 'icon' one could use to bring one object out from behind another and place it in the foreground. This is rather like the problem of the 'untrue' personality - one thing hidden behind another. Clearly the transposition of the two facets of personality cannot be dealt with by simply pressing a button, but if we are bold enough to question *everything,* we may well discover the means of bringing our true personality out into the foreground. Ask yourself these two simple questions..

Is being you really good enough?
Are you comfortable with YOU as you are?

An inadequate self image can easily produce feelings of both guilt and inferiority - feelings for which it is often difficult to account - endowing a person with a vague idea that they do not deserve good things to happen to them. Now this is *disastrous!* There is no other word for it. Earlier I mentioned destructive criticism and the effect it can have on a developing child. In adult life, the results of such childhood treatment may emerge as a 'fear' of success - but not just that. It may also be linked to an uneasy feeling of 'unworthiness'. If these feelings are present, there will often be a tendency to actually write off success as merely *luck* or *chance*, and to experience extreme discomfort and dis-ease when any form of public recognition arises.

If these remarks seem to ring small bells deep within you, do not despair! Help is at hand. There is a simple

FALSE LIMITATIONS...

technique for dispelling intrusive attitudes of the sort we have been discussing, and this we will come to a little later.

'I'll try...' is the precursor to one of the greatest of all false limitations. It might sound like a brave remark suggesting a real willingness to succeed. But beware! - *for it has provisional failure written all over it.* It is pre-empting failure and offering in advance the excuse that will probably be required. *'I'll try to catch the 6.30 train.'* A phrase like this is covering all the options for failure. It is tantamount to suggesting that you will probably miss the train.

These are simply examples of excusing possible failure in advance of the anticipated situation - and after all you have read so far, I am sure you will agree, this is not a very positive attitude! The use of phrases such as *'I'll try'* are attempts to smooth the way so that no blame will attach when non-achievement occurs.

Try always to be positive and make definite statements. *'I'll catch the 6.30.'* There is always the *possibility* that you might miss the train. But, by making a definite declaration, you are clearly going to make every attempt to catch it. Creating a cosy cocoon of possible failure around oneself will never develop a dynamic personality - and that is what is needed if success is to be the goal - *in anything you may choose to do in life.*

Say what you mean and mean what you say!
...and if you don't mean something, *don't say it!*

As we have seen, many personal limitations are the legacy of upbringing. Quite irrational fears may have been imposed on us and these will certainly limit what we feel we can achieve.

FALSE LIMITATIONS...

There is an amusing experiment you might like to try with a group of friends. Take a six foot length of timber, six inches wide, and place it on the floor, inviting someone to walk along it. No problem! Anyone can do this without even thinking about it. But now place the same length of timber supported between two chairs, so that it is about eighteen inches above the floor. Invite the same person to walk along it again. Many people will find it impossible!

Yet this is the same piece of timber, the same width and length - there was no thought of falling off it before, why should anything be different now? If you raised the timber even higher, there will be a limit when nobody would attempt to walk along it.

Why is a golfer so intimidated by a stretch of water or a bunker lying in his path? The shot he is about to make would offer no difficulties whatsoever if these obstacles were not there. But the distinct likelihood is a ball in the water or in the sand! Such false limitations are simply the workings of the mind, creating barriers that do not exist in reality.

The limitations we encounter which are the result of past experience and/or early training have the ability to affect our true potential. This is partly because we are fearful - or perhaps because we are intrinsically lazy.

We all have what are known as *comfort zones*. That is a quite understandable situation - except that there is a temptation for some people to reside within their comfort zone because they are too easily satisfied with their lot. They almost certainly lack ambition. They may never have tasted the good things of life, so are prepared to settle for the mediocre as the only state they know. If people are relatively content with the standards they have set themselves, there

FALSE LIMITATIONS...

seems to them little point in upsetting the status quo, so there is no incentive to make any great effort.

But this is not living!

Often those trapped by their own self-imposed limitations spend their lives vaguely grumbling without really knowing what is lacking in their life. Drive and ambition are the factors that are absent - a wish to experience something better. We all *need* to strive for something, to have goals and targets to stimulate ourselves into action. But the comfort zone is an ever-lurking danger, ready to embrace one in the cosy glow of relative success that will quickly stifle all further ambition, putting it on the back burner until further vague stirrings of dissatisfaction cause one to make another small effort.

Once snugly inside our comfort zone, the state of happy euphoria will impose its own particular brand of restriction by keeping alive feelings of unwarranted satisfaction derived from partial success and semi-achievement.

Our confidence depends so much on not feeling restricted, and in knowing that our achievements are observed and recognised by both our peers and our superiors. To be seen to be successful, even in a relatively small way, is of great motivational value. Each time we can repeat the experience, we are amplifying and strengthening our feelings of self-esteem. These experiences are the building blocks of personal growth.

Change rarely occurs in giant strides that are immediately obvious. Change takes place in a more subtle way, as a constant process, not unlike the growth of a plant. We cannot actually see a plant growing, and yet growth is taking place all the time - we are more inclined to notice the changes in that plant from time to time. Similarly personal growth is a

FALSE LIMITATIONS...

slow process involving the introduction and repetition of new ideas and practices, coupled with the suppression of unwanted attitudes and habits, all achieved through a constant *awareness* - an observation of *self.*

Stress, as I have already pointed out, is a word that has been given undue and unwarranted prominence in modern life. It has become a convenient hook on which to hang the blame for many personal short comings. We tend to talk of jobs and occupations with a high stress factor, but this may easily become a false limitation to our success because jobs and occupations do not themselves *represent* stress - for stress is a factor that human beings will manufacture for themselves. A job can involve a high level of *strain* - and there are many people quite able to accept that, without the *situation* itself actually being stressful.

Stress is yet another piece of excess baggage we should aim to discard on our journey towards change. Stress comes from *within,* it is not an external thing. Stress is the human response to an *external situation* - it is the way in which a human being perceives the *strain* that may be involved in that situation.

Viewed in the social context, stress is directly related to how self-conscious a person is, to how much other people's view of them actually matters to *them.* The way the world sees you will never be the same as the way you see yourself. But - and this is the crunch question - *how can you possibly know what the world, or any individual, thinks of you?* All you can know is *what you imagine* they think. We tend to worry far too much about such things, creating our own particular brand of self-inflicted stress, and through that, *imposing false limitations* upon ourselves.

FALSE LIMITATIONS...

We create our own external world through over working our imagination. Our personal world is not composed of *what is actually there* or *what is actually happening.* It is made up of what we *think* is there and what we *imagine* is happening. Harking back to the subconscious, just consider the part that it can play in this process of false image-building! To use an analogy, the structural drawing is there as a reality - we colour it the way we think or imagine it to be. Which brings me back, yet again, to the fundamental concept of this book - *that the world around us, as it affects us, is created by ourselves* - change *self* and that world is bound to change too.

'The mould of a man's fortune is in his own hands.'
Bacon (Essays) *'Of fortune'*

Positive action:

1. Ask yourself if you are existing in a comfort zone. If you think you are, set some new goals and strive towards new achievement.
Stretch yourself at all times and always aim for something just out of reach.

2. Considering the process of self-examination and self-appraisal, try to identify the areas of false limitation.

What is holding you back?
What are your in-built fears?
Are you sitting in a comfort zone of your own making?
If you feel you are - what do you think are the

FALSE LIMITATIONS...

factors that have created it? And how do you propose to climb out of it and continue your journey towards success and achievement?

Remember - *once an enemy is identified it becomes easier to defeat!*

11
Winners and losers

Any journey, no matter how long, begins with just a single step. That is a fact often quoted - and there is no escaping this simple truth.

It is the same for all of us, and yet there will always be those who arrive first, having completed the journey more easily than others and travelled along what appeared to be a different, simpler route. We perceive these people to be the natural winners in life. The rest seem somehow to get left far behind.

Is there some sort of natural selection involved in this? Are we divided naturally into winners and losers? Or is there something - some magic thing - that successful people do or have, or is it something they know or possess which evades the rest of the world?

Could it be luck? Could it be that certain people get all the opportunities, whilst the others are left out in the cold?

It is easy to identify successful people in all walks of life. It is not necessarily that they are better at what they do than the next man - it is that something about them ensures that they are always seen by others to be achievers. Others take notice of them - and they are successful because they believe that to be their natural state! They can see no reason why things should be otherwise.

They do not place stumbling blocks in their own path, and they do not recognise false limitations or consider, for a single moment, that they are unlikely to succeed. Indeed,

WINNERS AND LOSERS

they expect success! - they visualise themselves as being out in front of the pack, and anticipate nothing less than the winning position.

Those statements add up to just one thing - *successful people have a very highly developed sense of self-esteem.* Now some may interpret that as mere conceit. It is not. To have good feelings about yourself and to like yourself and realise your worth are necessary ingredients in the search for change, success and achievement.

Successful people are well aware of their personal uniqueness. Are they *really* unique? Yes they are - the fact is *we are all unique!*

Think about that - think about yourself. *You are totally unique* - there has never been anyone just like you before, and there will never be anyone just like you ever again. It is odd that most people in their wish to be anonymously absorbed into the great amorphous mass of humanity, do not recognise this. These are the naturally unambitious members of society who will probably never do anything exciting or remarkable because they lack any sense of their own uniqueness or worth. And yet, you know, these very people *do* have potential, for if we could find the means to fire their imagination and create a sense of excitement and urgency in them, they might be galvanised into the sort of action that could dramatically change their lives. Their special problem is that they have such a low level of self-esteem that it never occurs to them to visualise themselves in any kind of successful situation.

So now, perhaps, we are beginning to get an inkling of what makes successful people tick. They are not actually different to others, it is just that they have a particular view of themselves that is both positive and uncompromising. They *believe* in themselves and in their ability to succeed. They have decided what they want out of life, and are determined to get it. They have an instinctive understanding of *DE*, and of how to employ it, although they have probably never stopped to analyse just what it is. One other thing of which they are all aware - *success always demands its price.* No achievement comes without effort and dedication to an idea, often requiring sacrifice of time, expense, and personal freedom. Luck, should it enter the equation at all, is purely a bonus. Almost certainly *luck* will only have been the result of hard work and the ability to quickly recognise opportunity and respond to it.

Motivation and success are interchangeable elements which react one on the another. Motivation will normally precede success since it is the driving force. But, as we have seen, in the workings of *DE*, motivation can also be the product of success, stimulating and pushing one further, to even greater achievements and their attendant rewards - *success breeds success!*

We all have choice! It is for each of us to decide whether we take the route to success or the route leading to mediocrity and probable failure. *And it is always so much easier to fail!*

Nobody really knows what they are made of until they extend and stretch themselves towards the achievement of a higher goal than any they have so far experienced. The more we attempt to push back the boundaries of personal endeavour, the more we are likely to discover the latent capabilities of our own potential.

There was a time, not so many years ago, when it was unthinkable that a man could run a mile in four minutes. Roger Bannister truly believed it was possible and that he, with the aid of friends, was the man capable of proving it. As

WINNERS AND LOSERS

we know, he did it. He achieved what others thought impossible. Then because a new benchmark had been established, others recognised and accepted the challenge, pushing away the barriers even further, creating new records and setting new targets.

In 1953, on the day of Queen Elizabeth II's coronation, Edmund Hillary and Sherpa Tensing reached the top of Everest - a truly remarkable achievement. Yet, on one day in May 1992, 37 people did the same thing, representing a number of separate national expeditions!

Achievements of the calibre that both Bannister and Hillary demonstrated are the direct result of absolute self-belief, absolute faith in personal ability and absolute dedication to an idea - and that adds up to one thing - *focus*.

Never allow yourself to be put off by failure - your own or anyone else's. Failure is rarely an indication that success is not possible - and it is certainly not proof that something cannot be done. Rather it points out where you went wrong in your attempt, so that you may make the necessary adjustments that will carry you to eventual achievement. Consider the professional footballer. For every goal he scores, he will have made a dozen attempts which failed. Every shot at goal was *expected* to find its mark, but the footballer knows that to score every time simply is not possible. If he allowed his mistakes and inaccuracies to get him down, he would not last very long in the game. He has learned to make positives out of negatives. He operates on the basis of *expectation*. Each missed shot increases his determination to succeed - and he does.

We must learn to turn adversity to our own advantage.

WINNERS AND LOSERS

Shakespeare, as usual, found just the right words...

'Sweet are the uses of adversity, which like the toad, ugly and venomous, wears yet a precious jewel in its head.'
'As you like it'

Bannister's attainment on the running track was real success, motivated in the right way through a burning *desire* for the achievement of a very personal goal. Today the sports scene is greatly changed. As more and more records are smashed, and scientific advances produce timing equipment with an accuracy undreamed of only a few years ago, competition - *who wins or who loses* - often turns on micro fractions of a second. Training and motivation of the highest order is the only way that the split second challenge can be met. And yet we still hang on to this idea of winners and losers. To win, implies that someone else loses, and our perception of a loser is of someone who is not quite good enough. The difference between the two, in the modern context of super-sport, may be no more than a one hundredth of a second!

It is common practice at motivational seminars and gatherings to present super-sports men and women as examples of true achievement and as *winners* to be idolised and emulated. Such people are certainly to be admired as individuals who went out into the world with the burning idea of excelling in their own particular speciality, and succeeded spectacularly. But that success does not imply that they have necessarily become better and more complete human beings, simply because they can run faster, jump further, or hit harder than the rest of us. It is no fault of theirs that others want to place them on a pedestal!

WINNERS AND LOSERS

I was once bored to tears at a convention by a lady cricketer whose laddish swearing was presumably calculated to impress her male audience, and, on another occasion, by a football manager of international reputation, so foul-mouthed as to be downright embarrassing. I have been variously embarrassed or bored by a host of other sporting personalities, presented as public speakers, whose only claim to fame was their particular brilliance at a particular sport - certainly not at public speaking! They had done their best in their chosen occupation and achieved the goals they had set their hearts on. It is the fault of others that these innocent achievers get thrust into the limelight - seduced, probably, by hefty fees - and are expected to perform to standards that frankly are beyond their capabilities.

It would, I think, be difficult to find any dictionary definition of *success* that made any mention of beating others. Winning and losing are merely manifestations of the degree of ability one individual - or group (team) - has related to a specific accomplishment, over another individual or group.

Success and competition are not synonymous - competition as a stimulus to effort can be a fine thing - but the idea of struggling to be No.1 is an encouragement to see everyone else as second best, and that cannot be what life is all about. Personal success should be a part of personal development - an enhancement to and an enrichment of personality. Remember your utter uniqueness! Once you can accept that as a fact, why should there ever be any need to compare yourself with others? Competition *is* making comparisons - pointing out that one person is better than another, and by making such comparisons you could be planting the seeds of envy - and that can never be of any benefit.

WINNERS AND LOSERS

By all means take the way others work and use it as a role model to emulate if you must, but be sure that those you wish to copy are worthy of imitation! - especially in the field within which *you* operate. The sense of your own very special uniqueness is the best starting point you could ever have. Build on that and develop a real attitude of self-esteem - an attitude that will eventually allow you to realise that all things are possible, and that it is not necessary to compare yourself with *anyone!* The truth is that success is not a matter of comparing oneself with others, so much as *comparing oneself with oneself* - with one's own developing capabilities, as well as past achievements.

Success is an internal happening more than something to be observed. It requires work and attention, *focus* and *awareness* at all times. It is persuading our subconscious to accept the concept that we are loveable and worthwhile people, capable of great things through our total uniqueness and highly developed sense of self-esteem. Now *there's* something for it to get to work on!

12

Success

Success is counted sweetest
By those who ne'er succeed...
- Emily Dickenson 1830-1886

If your idea of success is beating others, you are almost certainly starting your journey on the wrong foot!

Success implies different things to each one of us, but the truly successful person knows just what its precise meaning is to him or her. Successful people see no possibility of failure because they use the power of imaging and positive thinking to build and sustain their self-image.

Success cannot exist in isolation - by that I mean it cannot be confined to, or relative to just one area of life. It is an all-embracing notion, colouring everything and everyone it touches. When the whole of one's life can be enriched as a direct result of the sustained effort necessary to achieve a particular goal, that is success of a high order.

Success is a complicated compound of many ingredients. The idea of success is, in its many-faceted definition, relative to age, circumstance and environment. To a child it may be the acquisition of a longed-for bicycle, or getting into a school team. To a teenager it may be having a date with a very special person. To an adult it might be surrounding oneself with all the trappings and visible status symbols of other people's perception of success. To an elderly retired person it may be no more than successfully getting to the local shops

SUCCESS

and back again. Whatever it might be, there are always two vital common denominators -
the setting and achievement of goals.

Success is definable as the knowledge that separates the achievers from the rest - I was tempted to say the *winners from the losers*, but in the light of everything I have already said, that would have been strictly out of order! To be a *loser* implies that one has striven and failed - and failure is far from being the same thing as non-achievement - probably the result of indolence, disinterest, or simply a lack of suitable motivation.

Providing that one approaches a task with the right attitude, success will almost certainly be its predictable outcome. In the most blatantly simplistic terms, striving for success comes down to knowing exactly what one must do - *and then doing it!*

Some years ago in the United States there was an investigation into the reasons for the tremendous turn-over of sales men and women in the life assurance business. Two thousand people who had left the industry responded to a comprehensive questionnaire, and out of the evaluation of the vast amount of information, came one simple fact - 80% of all those questioned, answered, *'nobody told me what to do.'* The head of training for a large insurance company in this country told me that the reason for a similar high drop-out rate here, was *'they simply don't do what they have been told to do.'* Confusing, isn't it?

How many truly successful people do you know? We have become accostomed to perceiving public figures such as politicians, entertainers, sportsmen, TV personalities, as successful people. But, very often their success lies in just one small area of their lives - the area for which they have become known to the general public, the area that has brought them significant wealth. Many of these people only excel because they are doing *the only thing they know and understand.* They are obsessive about their occupation, or about the skills they have learned, as a means of achieving their fame and fortune. The result, of course, is success of a kind - it would be churlish to deny that - but it is not always success of the all-embracing kind of which we have been speaking.

Many sports super-stars are trained and encouraged to develop what is known as a *killer instinct.* Their emotions can become quite excessive - totally unrelated to the real world. The aim is to wipe out the opposition, and, through that, the task of winning can assume proportions which obliterate most normal human values. So obsessive can some people become through over training and the resultant distorted reasoning, that *losing* actually becomes a very painful experience. A well-known tennis star, at his performance peak, was a prime example of the ultimate in positive mental attitude, but being an emotional person, the exaggerated height of mental preparation was probably what caused his famous explosions on the court. Following these outbursts, having himself been blown apart by his own gross behaviour, he was apparently overcome by remorse.

We have all heard of the archetype comedian who, off stage, is a tragic figure - sad, morose, unfulfilled and disgruntled. Or the millionaire who enjoys little of life and is, all too often, ready and willing to take advantage of others simply to gain some small financial advantage.

Yet people take great pleasure in saying - having met some well-known celebrity - that he or she *was so nice, so*

SUCCESS

genuine! Could it be that we do not expect famous and successful people to possess those attributes? *'Their success hasn't spoilt them a bit!'* Why on earth should it? - if anything, it should have *improved* them!

Our unconscious perception of success is closely related to the *win/lose* philosophy, by which people are out to defeat one another. True success should, if it has any worth at all, bring added value to most areas of life, as well as having the ability to touch others in a way that will enrich their lives too.

The truly successful person is in a privileged position. He or she can afford to look around and observe the beneficial affects they can have on the lives of others. They have no need to take advantage of anyone, but can, if they so desire, share their success with others by making spontaneous gestures of generosity without any need of recognition. What a truly splendid state...

> *'The mind is its own place, and in it self can make a Heav'n of Hell, a Hell of Heav'n.'*
> **- Milton**

Naturally successful people are bristling with observable assets:

They are keen and anxious to learn.
They will listen.
They ask questions and demand comprehensive answers.
They are thinking people, displaying active curiosity.
They are genuinely interested in others, and are always willing to help those less fortunate than themselves.
They understand the importance of goal-setting -
Therefore they achieve their aims.
They are not afraid of displaying genuine emotion.

SUCCESS

They have a quick and ready empathy.
They have great enthusiasm.
They are very positive in their approach to life.
Their lives are not bounded by *if*, but rather by *when*.
They like to see *everybody* win, rather than have winners and losers.

Life strikes no bargains and makes no promises or guarantees. All one can hope to do is one's very best, but always *with an attitude of total expectation*.

There is nothing to be gained by *wishing*, and grumbling over not having had the breaks, or not having been given the opportunities from which others have been able to benefit. Success comes through *expectation*, coupled with the knowledge that you have certain capabilities, and believing that you have it in your power to be successful. There must be a genuine *desire* to succeed, for without that little will come about. You get out of life what you *expect* to get, not simply what you *want*. The person who can see no reason why they should not be able to accomplish something has the greatest chance of real achievement.

The creative ability of a child is based, as we have already seen, on innocent *expectation*. A child doesn't sit back and wonder *how* to do something. It *assumes* it can do it! - *and does it* in a completely natural and uninhibited way.

There is no correlation between success and intelligence or the education one may have enjoyed. It is more to do with *belief* - for with belief, all things are possible.

    'If you believe you can do a thing,
or if you believe you cannot - you are right!'
— **Henry Ford**

SUCCESS

It is easier to create barriers to success than it is to remove them. As we have seen, we are capable of placing every stumbling block in our own path to hold ourselves back and restrict our potential. Man himself is the greatest barrier to his own achievement! But, if we have acquired the habit of belief and developed a good self-image, we will easily see our way forward, demolish the barriers and break down all self-imposed restriction. *Belief* can carry us to the farthest and most exciting areas of life.

The power of belief can be quite extraordinary. The witch doctor in a primitive society has total sway over his people, even to holding power over life and death. The people's belief in his powers is so complete that, should he tell one of them they are going to die, they surely will. In modern medicine, too, belief has an important role to play, sometimes contributing more to the curative or healing process than the practitioner or his treatment. The psychology of the placebo - a harmless medication given to a patient, usually used in a controlled trial - is that a cure may often be affected simply because the patient *believes* that the expected medicine was administered.

Belief, hope and expectation are strongly linked. We are very much the masters of our destiny so far as expectations go. What you expect to get out of life, you will inevitably get. *Not what you want* - but what you *expect!*

Expectations can easily become our own self-fulfilling prophesies. Going back to healing, and the process of recovery from illness, if the patient has no belief, but rather, displays an attitude of hopelessness, they place themselves in a dangerous situation. The image of *no recovery* can actually kill, such is the power of the mind.

SUCCESS

So, *be positive!* Expect the good things of life to come your way because you deserve them, and they will surely abound. Expect the worst and it will almost certainly come your way.

Believe in the power of your own positive thinking!

The expectations - both good and bad - that a parent may have for a child can have great influence on the child's development, and particularly on the attitudes the child may carry into later life. If parental attitudes were over-critical, the child, in adult life, might well have a tendency to hold back, reflecting a lack of belief in his or her own ability. Conversely, the positive, loving and supportive parent with a healthy expectation of their child's ability will, almost certainly, foster a natural success. Sigmund Freud made the interesting observation that great men often had doting mothers, and it was this adulation that gave them the confidence to attempt great things.

So, how much controlling power does your past still exert on you? Once you can understand and rationalise this you can begin the process of improving and developing a self-image that will no longer inhibit your natural progress in your quest for a more successful you.

The majority of human beings have an instinctive craving for achievement. We all want to be good at something. We know how good it makes us feel, and it is as natural to want success as it is to wish to stay alive. By now, I sincerely hope that you have got the feeling that everyone really does have the potential to achieve anything they want to do. The basic problem is that there are far too few people capable of actually imagining themselves as being successful, probably because they have never really experienced the feelings of real achievement, so have little idea of what an exciting thing

SUCCESS

success can be. To have earned the recognition of one's peers is a most satisfying experience, but it is just as important to know the inner feelings that go with it, for retaining and remembering such feelings will always help you when striving towards future goals. Try always to recall the feelings you experienced when *DE* was operating - this is the feeling that precedes success and achievement.

Learn the art of keeping the control centre inside yourself, not allowing it to be dominated or influenced by outside agencies.

Is success related to ability? To a certain extent, yes, but since ability is no more than the acquisition of skill, some other element is needed to achieve the desired end result - success. It is ability that, in a purely physical sense, carries us forward to the satisfactory conclusion of a task, but no matter how able an individual may be, success will not be its necessary or logical outcome. As Napoleon said... *ability is of little account without opportunity.*

Opportunity lies all around you - it is just a matter of recognising it, pinning it down, and generating massive action. The person who sits around intellectualising over the pros and cons of an opportunity will see it pass him by. Opportunities must be seized and acted on speedily, bringing all one's abilities to the task - and there is a simple recipe for success.

What about the *appearance* of success? Most of us recognise a successful person by their demeanour and general appearance. The person who dresses well and looks successful, will usually be accepted as *being* successful. *You only have one chance to make a first impression* - worth remembering if you are operating in an environment where

SUCCESS

appearance can influence outcome. It has been observed that during an election the better presented candidate will attract most votes. Well turned out job applicants will be taken more notice of than those who have not taken much trouble over their appearance. Presenting yourself as a well-packaged proposition can make the difference between success or failure in a job interview.

One of the most significant social changes that has taken place in recent years is the sweeping away of 'dress code' barriers. It is no longer easy to identify or categorise people in terms of occupation, education, or social origins. There is a new and welcome universality in the way people tend to dress, making it almost impossible to pick up many of the visual clues that, in the past, could reveal so much.

A great deal of nonsense has been written about the psychological aspects of dressing, and the messages that may be presented. Dark suits, for example, are said to command feelings of respect and confidence and are generally seen as more dignified than suits in lighter colours. Women - and I would not dare to trespass far into this field! - tend to have a much better sense of occasion and suitability to purpose than their male counterparts!

... if you dress like a slob, soon you begin to think like a slob - and before long, you will act like a slob!

Positive action:

1. Ask yourself what sort of image you present to the world? Look at yourself very critically, and write down how you feel others would describe you.

2. Now write down how you would describe yourself

to someone who had never seen you. How well do the two descriptions coincide?

3. Consider your best attributes, and make a list of them. Make another list cataloguing your least attractive features!

4. Now write out another description - how you would like to be *able* to describe yourself.

13

Change - and the power of the unseen

The energy produced by our minds radiates out like the beam from a lighthouse, and the effects can be felt, sometimes even at a considerable distance, by others who are in tune with us. You may recall the example earlier in the book of the painter on the verge of an exhibition.

Most of us have had the experience of thinking about someone who, seemingly miraculously, has immediately contacted us. This is clearly the result of some form of telepathic communication. As with so many things in life, this power has the possibility of working in more than one direction - it can have both a positive or a negative influence. Negative thoughts, if sufficiently strong, have the power to attract negative circumstances - this is what we often label as a self-fulfilling prophesy. It is possible to literally think ourselves into a detrimental situation through the power of our own imagination. At any time it is possible for our most dominant thought patterns, good or bad, to attract similar feelings. This is the process of *resonance*, to which I have already referred.

So, the world around you - your external world - is simply a reflection, a product even, of your inner state - *of what is happening in your own mind.* This is a very powerful concept...and what amazing power it embodies. It allows for the possibility of changing the world immediately *around* you, by changing the world *within* you. You have the ability to change and affect relationships, and to influence the way in which people perceive and treat you. This action is simply a reflection of your own personality and your own attitudes. If you are able to modify the way in which you behave towards others, you will certainly be treated by them in a similar manner. *As you sow, so shall you reap...*

The implications of all we have discussed so far must be, by now, becoming abundantly clear. Perhaps you believe in destiny as a force over which we have little control - something that lies beyond the scope of our influence. Only you can decide what you feel about that.

However, the one thing you *can* control is what goes on in your own mind and therefore, as we have seen, through that there is definite potential for influencing the circumstances that surround you. It is the *quality* of that influence that is the key to how well you will be able to guide the direction of your own life. It may be that destiny does indeed control us, and that particular aspects of our journey are mapped out, but as with all journeys, there is always the possibility of deviation. We might inadvertently stray from the chosen path and wander off down what may prove to be nothing more than a cul-de-sac. From time to time we will be confronted by forks in the road, points at which we have the opportunity to make a life-altering decision. The fact is we *are* offered these chances to influence our own destiny and to determine the quality of the life we wish to lead. This concept of destiny and potential is very like the pre-conceived picture and the idea that the painting only becomes truly creative as mistakes occur - mistakes that alter the original planned course, bringing life and originality to the final result.

Man is constantly trying to bring change to the world about him - not always with the greatest success in so far as it affects

CHANGE - AND THE POWER OF THE UNSEEN

his own life. As we have seen, if man's desire is to achieve change within his own life, it is he that must change first. Our surrounding world is merely a product of our own imaginative perception. We may only bring about change to our personal view of that world by attempting to straighten out the distortions we have deliberately or accidentally created. Alter your own inner world and you will be astounded at the way the external world appears to respond.

No doubt you have heard of *Positive Mental Attitude* - or PMA, as it is often known. This is a power not concerned with *wanting* or *wishing,* but with *expectation.*

At this moment, you are the sum total of everything you have ever been told, thought or experienced, with all the in-built positives and negatives that are part of the territory. The purpose of our journey together is to 'edit' that life, to discard all that is useless and unnecessary, so as to make room for better attitudes and ideas that will enrich and embellish life from this point onwards. We may need to make some minor adjustments to the steering gear of our frail vessel, so as to enable us to steer a straight course towards some new goals.

You now know where the changes have to take place - *in your own mind.* There is one word that sums up everything - *belief* - a word to keep constantly in the forefront of your mind. It has the starring role in the process of achieving your new mental attitude, and will colour everything you do. It embodies the notion of belief in yourself as well as belief in the possibility of real change. It underlines the fact that all things are possible and can be achieved through this new outlook on life.

CHANGE - AND THE POWER OF THE UNSEEN

Let us now return to the idea that our minds are machines operating on two levels. On one level is the conscious mind with which we think and reason, whilst the second level is that which is controlling our daily activity and dealing with all the complicated nitty-gritty related to simply being and staying alive. This part of the brain is performing millions of functions every second as it activates each movement we make, every action we take. Computer-like, it never ceases translating every thought, sight, sound and sensation into action through the process of comparative assessment coupled to the provision of endless feed-back.

It is positively breathtaking to consider what we can achieve - and the processes involved are active all the time. Think of driving a car whilst listening to music and thinking about the problems of everyday life. How often have you reached a destination without remembering much about the journey, the situations you negotiated, the actions you took - and yet you arrived safely? Consider the mental processes that went on during that journey: the computations of speed, distance, time and braking power that took place quite spontaneously. Action followed action, whilst another part of the brain responded to the music and, at the same time, rambled amongst the problems of the day. The actions required and the messages sent and received that made the journey possible were all activated at the subconscious level of the brain - that 'bio-computer' that is forever comparing past and present experiences - producing what we think of as automatic responses and actions. This is not the rational, reasoning part of the brain, but the part that only reacts to *instructional programming*. You may marvel at the computer on your desk, but it is an amateur compared to the miraculous thing inside your head which you take totally for granted.

CHANGE - AND THE POWER OF THE UNSEEN

There are people who live their lives literally engineering their own failures, simply because they were programmed with restrictive attitudes right from day one. If you can recognise this situation in yourself and can see just how unsatisfactory it is, and you can believe that better things could prevail, your immediate job is to unscramble the muddle you have so far lived with and begin the process of re-programming so as to become the person you would truly like - and *expect* - to be.

Staying with the computer analogy, properly prepared programming instructions must be produced to ensure that the machine can perform the tasks and functions expected of it. These instructions are fed into the computer's memory so that every action it takes is the direct result of planned commands. It is amazing how often one hears people blaming computers for mistakes. Computers *do not make mistakes* - that is the exclusive preserve of the human being! Programmers and operators make mistakes...

At the subconscious level the human mind works in much the same way as the computer. It is not - just as a computer is not - a thinking mechanism. It is a mechanism that responds to commands, and can only function on the basis of the information with which it is provided. It is incapable of being logical or critical - that is *your* function, based on the assessments with which you are provided by the subconscious. The more precise the information passing in either direction, the better and more effective will be the outcome. This is the process that we have come to know as *learning*.

Programming entails emptying out the unnecessary commands that relate to the producion of out-dated and unwanted conditioned responses, and replacing these with new commands that will help to develop *the habit of success* as an instinct.   Army training is an excellent example of programming. Discipline is achieved through endless *rehearsal* (training) which produces an instant, unquestioning response. Under pressure, and in perhaps severely dangerous conditions, it is essential that every man will react in a precisely predictable manner. His life and the lives of his comrades may depend on his actions, and it is only training - *endless rehearsal* - that can produce this all-important automatic disciplined response.

It is precisely the same with our quest for change and success in life. We must train ourselves to the concepts that represent what we want to achieve. Learning processes are really no more than rehearsals, so that, just like the soldier on the battlefield, actions and responses become automatic.

At the beginning of this book I suggested that you get rid of all the excess baggage in your life - everything, in fact, that is of no further use or benefit to you. This included clothes which you are never likely to wear again, and all the other extraneous junk that we tend to hoard, 'just in case'!

WELL! - DID YOU DO IT ?

The suggestion was a preliminary exercise - something to make you feel good, as well as something to put you into a receptive frame of mind before you delved too far into the book. But, *I wonder if you actually did it...*

We are now back to clearing out time again! The moment has arrived when we should start clearing out the dusty recesses of the mind - everything, in fact, that is of no further use or benefit. The very first thing we are going to discard is that awful *could-do-better* label. You know perfectly well

CHANGE - AND THE POWER OF THE UNSEEN

that you have always been capable of doing better. Why else would you be reading this book?

So, let us now look at the procedures we must employ, and the ground rules we must follow to ensure that *best* becomes the norm, *the permanent state* - not something which is never quite attained.

Do you feel that you are a completely unique individual?

I want you to consider this question quite seriously. Out of the entire population of the world, you could be identified by finger prints, blood group, voice print, and most certainly by DNA testing. These are all means of identifying a human being with both precision and exactitude. That surely must make you totally unique?

But it doesn't! Those are merely scientific ways of cataloguing your physical uniqueness, almost by a process of elimination. To be unique because of a series of features over which you have no possible control is no real claim to individuality! Finger prints and all the other paraphernalia of identification represent no more than the name and address on the package. This shell within which we live is only a vehicle that we conveniently inhabit so as to carry around the really unique bits of ourselves - *the mind and the soul.*

Do you feel that you are in control of your own life?
and/or
Do you feel that external circumstances dominate you?
Is your life over shadowed by debts, occupation, your boss and/or your own state of health?

If these questions pin-point your situation, something has got a little out of proportion, and the evidence suggests that *your*

CHANGE - AND THE POWER OF THE UNSEEN

centre of control lies, as it were, outside your body. This is a state which allows no scope at all for flexibility, creativity or any potential for beneficial development. External circumstances should never be allowed to dominate, as there are always better things within to occupy that special position.

It is thoughts and expectations that are most likely to affect our actions. Clearly, the power centre of control must be reinstated on the *inside*. If external elements are controlling you, then life will be no more than a dull struggle, both worrisome and mundane. The successful person - the higher achiever - is a far happier, better balanced and more self-fulfilled person because he has kept the control centre *within* himself.

And what about your emotions? Are you happy, sad, excited, fearful, apprehensive? Your behaviour at any specific point in time will be governed by your thought patterns. *Do you agree with that statement?*

Your actions then, are the result of your thoughts. Is it not logical to suggest that, if you are in control of your thoughts, you are also in control of your actions, and are therefore determining the way your life is shaping and moving - as well as the way in which that outer world responds to you? By the same token, if you have lost control of your thoughts - implying that control has reverted to the outside - your actions will be unpredictable, unplanned and utterly haphazard. That is a process that can never lead to any kind of satisfactory fulfilment or self-improvement.

Remember that you become *what you think*, so it is important to do everything you can to make certain your thinking is right! After all, what is thinking but *planning*?

CHANGE - AND THE POWER OF THE UNSEEN

We spend most of our time talking to ourselves, carrying on a constant dialogue between our conscious thinking mind and our subconscious - the data bank of experience. And we know that the subconscious willingly accepts all it is told. Because of this, you must see how important it is to remain positive at all times, so that the right attitudes are passed down the line.

Never make any declaration to yourself about yourself that you would not wish to become a reality.

Avoid making negative or destructive statements. As I have already mentioned, there is a negative chemistry that can affect the body as a result of negative thoughts, and this can certainly attract the very things that you fear or dislike most. *I* - as in *I can't* or *I will try,* or even *I am tired* - is the trigger to make your subconscious sit up and take notice. *I* is recognised as the signal that precedes a command or a personal statement. Everything that follows *I* will be seriously recorded and filed away, if not acted upon immediately.

I have already discussed the influence parents and teachers may have on children in their formative years, and how, as a result of programmed attitudes, certain embedded patterns of behaviour have been carried right into adult life. Many of these influences will have been beneficial, whilst others may have left feelings of hurt which are very difficult to forgive and forget. Others, again, may have even been influences of evil.

In the times in which we live there is a very definite and obvious tendency for parents, especially those who are socially and economically disadvantaged, to disregard the notion of *responsibility* to or for their children, and to society in general. Brought up under such influences is it any wonder that delinquency is so rife among the young? Parents, at best and worst, are role models, and have the greatest influence through example. But, as we keep observing, there is always a positive and a negative side to every attribute. The good or bad influence of parents is a very strong aspect of the initial programming of young people. The first seven years of a child's life establishes the pattern for both character and behavioural patterns. With young people entering society who are programmed with feelings representing total irresponsibility, coupled with many other bad influences, what hope is there for the generation they will themselves bring into the world? If any of these thoughts ring bells within your own experience, the time has certainly come to redress that balance.

We need to develop an attitude of conscious forgiveness if we are to successfully clear out the effects of past programming from our minds and become fully functioning adults. If you have been harbouring grudges or feelings of blame, you must let them go completely. An enemy recognised is an enemy defeated. It might actually help if you say out loud...*'I completely forgive so-and-so'*. The important thing is that you are able to cast off any feelings of resentment or disappointment you may have always felt towards certain people, and the best way of achieving this is to really lay it on the line by voicing your feelings out loud - but always with thoughts and expressions of *total forgiveness*. Believe me, you will experience nothing but good feelings by doing this.

This simple act doesn't really have much to do with the other person - indeed, they are *probably* unaware of any of

CHANGE - AND THE POWER OF THE UNSEEN

the feelings you may have been unconsciously harbouring - unless, that is, they gather some hint of your feelings telepathically.

The very personal actions you are engaging in are concerned with deep-seated emotions. You are carrying out actions which will nourish and enrich your own peace of mind, and will, almost certainly, have a profound effect on the process of change we are aiming to achieve.

You may never have thought about these things, but do you feel that *you* could be to blame for some of the attitudes that colour your everyday life? Could *you* be responsible for the person you have become? If this is the case, *then forgive yourself too!* Forgive yourself - out loud - for all the foolish deeds, indiscretions and follies you have perpetrated, all the wrong directions you may have taken. Forgive yourself totally, and then, having done that - *forget it!*

In the attempt to straighten out our thinking, we are dealing with two elements - two polarities, in fact. *Desires* and *fears*.

Desires are not the same as wishes which, as we have seen, are no more than hazy hopes - loosely directed toward some half-defined ideal. *Desire,* on the other hand, is the solid fuel needed to drive us towards achievement. It is, as we already know, the starting point to every ambitious aspiration. The stronger the desire, coupled with the belief that achievement is possible, the more certain will be the outcome. We could give a new name to this equation...

$$desire + belief = focus.$$

The real key to change, then, is to keep your mind totally focused to make it impossible for the negative element of *fear* to creep in and create doubt. Most fears are the deeply buried and 'forgotten' legacies of upbringing, the triggers that, as we have observed, activate conditioned responses. It is these fears that can make us feel unaccountably uneasy, even unhappy, whilst desires, as you might expect, tend to stimulate us.

It seems to me - and I am not a psychologist - that to simply try to repress unwanted feelings is doing no more than making sure we retain them, by pushing them deeper into the subconscious. We know that anything that remains in that repository has a nasty habit of resurfacing without warning or invitation in the future. As Franklin D Roosevelt once said, *'the only thing we have to fear is fear itself'*. So, how do we set about combating fear? Negative feelings and thoughts can only be conquered by *replacement* with much stronger, more positive, vibrant emotions. In the quest for success, there can be no possible thought of failure, for that would be allowing an attitude of doubt to sneak into our thoughts. Your own desire to succeed is the greatest weapon in your armoury. Desire has the power to overcome everything providing the emotion is sufficiently strong and the *focus* is total. You must consciously encourage your mind to become so obsessed with your expectations and with the feelings you know you will experience through your ultimate achievement, that there will be no time at all for it to dwell on unimportant fears and worries.

14

Desire, belief and expectation

As we grow older, and hopefully more mature, we tend to become increasingly self-directed. That is not to say, of course, that we become any wiser. At the same time, in our general development, energy levels begin to diminish as we approach what is generally presumed to be our optimum potential.

In everyone's working life there is a time at which they peak. This will usually be just before reaching that point that can be justifiably labelled their *level of incompetence.* As with all peaks, the only way is down - for up is no longer an available option. This pattern is likely to coincide with what we vaguely refer to as middle age - a dangerous period in the cycle of a person's life - because the familiarity with occupation is beginning to dull the edge of interest and enthusiasm. It is also the time when redundancy can start to loom in the distance as a distinct possibility.

The best years of their lives are behind such a person, and even though experience and reliability are valuable assets, it is all too common for the middle aged to get chopped out of the system, in favour of a younger, more active person - and this at a time in life when such a happening can represent very severe blow.

Employers gain comfort and solace from the use of such phrases as *natural wastage* or *early retirement.* These are merely contrivances to make them feel less like the villain of the piece.

DESIRE, BELIEF & EXPECTATION

In middle age - especially if redundancy is likely to occur - it is very difficult to define new goals or to focus on any sort of new directional thrust. The rudderless ship - a situation that can so easily lead to a state of utter despair and hopelessness. You may possibly have experienced such a situation. You will almost certainly know someone who has.

If redundancy has been your own experience, it is to be hoped that you have been able to pick yourself up, dust yourself down and to make a fresh start. *Appendix 3* at the end of the book continues the redundancy theme with, I hope, some useful thoughts.

Goal setting can have many beneficial effects. For example, a state of inertia and hopelessness will quickly dissipate as soon as a new sense of direction can be found. Goals will always trigger behavioural patterns, and their consequences will maintain them, so goal-setting is in an important building process, aimed at speeding recovery and generating activity. By degrees self-confidence will return, amplified by the desire for and the belief in the ability to completely turn things around. Soon the faculty which allows one to identify and solve problems will reappear as the motivational level rises towards the point where *DE* inevitably starts to operate. Expectation of achievement can be a wonderfully uplifting experience!

Everyone is a potential success. However, for one reason or another - but hopefully only on a purely temporary basis - some people are disguised as failures! Most likely this will be the fault of some totally unexpected happening, or simply the backlash from past influences. Our immediate task, then, is to produce our 'programme' on the basis of goals and

DESIRE, BELIEF & EXPECTATION

expectations - and there must be nothing vague, negative or indeterminate about this.

At some time or other we have all indulged in dreaming of the things we would like to possess, the places we would like to visit, and the lifestyle we would like to enjoy. Dreams of this nature are actually rather negative self-indulgences, rooted as they so often are in the envy of other people's success and achievement. *Wishes* often express unconscious personal doubts of the *'if only'* variety. They are usually based on a lack of confidence, on not really believing that the attainment of such things is within the dreamer's reach. Wishing is no more than hoping, and hope is simply clinging to the vagueness of possibility.

So, considering these somewhat frail and negative factors, how likely is it that these dreams will ever become a reality? Remote chance is the only answer one can give, unless, that is, we could formulate an approach - an attitude - that allows all things to become possible. We now know enough to recognise that three key words are missing from the notions we have been considering above. They are, of course, *desire, belief,* and *expectation.*

Anything the human mind can conceive and believe in
<u>is achievable</u>

That sentence sums up what people like to call *the secret of success.*

All attempts at change or self-improvement must begin with desire, belief and expectation. For example, to give up smoking (see *Appendix 2*) need not be as difficult as most people think, providing that is, they have a real *desire* to kick the habit.

DESIRE, BELIEF & EXPECTATION

By all means, go on having daydreams about the things you really want, either in the way of tangible goods, or as achievements, but <u>drop from your vocabulary</u> the words *wish* and *hope*. Replace them with *desire, belief* and *expectation*. When you can truly make this adjustment to your thinking, *all things are possible!*

This is not such an easy adjustment to make. To move from the negative to the positive, there may be many stages through which one must pass...

      100% - *I did!*
      90% - I will...
      80% - I can...
      70% - I think I can...
      60% - I might...
      50% - I think I might...
      40% - Could I?
      30% - I wish I could...
      20% - I don't know how...
      10% - I can't...
      0% - *I won't!*

Looking at this staircase, climbing as it does, from *doubt* to *total realisation*, we can see very clearly just how far apart the polarities of negative and positive really are.

Because you are reading this book, you are obviously interested in change. Notice I said *interested in*. By now it should be abundantly clear that you must *desire* change if anything is going to be achieved. All your desired changes must be identified, recognised and pinned down very

DESIRE, BELIEF & EXPECTATION

precisely in writing, then set out clearly as a series of personal goals.

The subconscious has no sense of time and does not reason. It simply acts on information received. Some motivational writers suggest that goals should always be expressed as though they have already been achieved. I have my doubts about this practice because, by implanting the suggestion that the achievement has been accomplished, when, in fact, it is still no more than a desire, could produce a confusion both in the conscious and the subconscious mind. We need to be very clear and precise in the way we express goals in writing.

Always make goals ambitious, a little stretching, yet realisable. Express them as clearly and in as much detail as possible. The better the directions and instructions, the more likely it is that the astounding mechanism within you will be awakened to possibility and show itself able to produce results.

The setting of a time-scale is important to goal. All goals need to be pinned down by the addition of a time limit for their achievement. Most people have heard of *'Parkinson's Law'*, one variant of which suggests that *any task will take up the amount of time allocated to it.* With this in mind, keep time-scales short but realistic when expressing the requirements of your goal.

There is one very important thing to remember when setting goals down in writing. *How* a goal is to be achieved is no concern of yours at this stage. Your subconscious will deal with that, and assuming your desires and beliefs are real, the directional answers will come to you in their own way, by the emergence of sudden ideas, flashes of inspiration, hunches, and so on. But, and this is very important, *you*

DESIRE, BELIEF & EXPECTATION

must be prepared to follow the advice you receive. This is where true belief comes in - *there is no point in keeping a dog and barking yourself!*

<u>At this stage - a personal note to my reader...</u>

I would not be in the least surprised if, at this point, you are beginning to experience a certain scepticism! And why not? If you have never encountered ideas of this sort before, scepticism is a perfectly understandable reaction.

All manner of people will read this book, and some of the ideas and concepts it presents will definitely lack appeal. This does not matter one bit. The book is simply suggesting options that are open to all of us - if we want to take them up. It is better to be confronted with ideas that one can reject than never to have thought about them at all.

It seems to be symptomatic of modern life that the book shops are full of volumes on self-improvement, success, achievement, winning, and becoming something you are not, but would like to be! And, of course, the book you are reading is no exception! But has anyone, I wonder, ever considered writing a book on failure? If they have, no doubt it would be analysing what failure is and demonstrating how to turn things around to become a success!

I hope very much that having read this far you will have an idea of the potential that lies within each one of us. The ideas I am putting forward are intended to awaken your consciousness and to enable you to benefit from a great power available to all of us, which can start the process of regeneration and reconstruction.

Knowing one's limitations is important in every aspect of life. It represents the line that divides happiness in achievement from the sadness of failure.

DESIRE, BELIEF & EXPECTATION

No matter what I may write or you may read, it is the enjoyment of life that should be everyone's constant aim. To some people, striving to be the best will supply all the satisfaction and reward they need to achieve fulfilment. The perpetual adrenaline drive is all they ask.

The attempt at any sort of change or modification is to embark on a most exciting journey, and, as with any journey, the unexpected can always occur, so there is a need to be alert and always to remain receptive to possibilities which could lead one down new and even more interesting routes.

I have lead you to the beginning of the real path. From now on the journey must be your own exploration, and you will certainly discover new routes for yourself, often, it would seem, by chance. Remember though - when the pupil is ready, the teacher will appear.

> *This above all, to thine own self be true*
> *And it must follow as the night the day,*
> *Thou cans't not then be false to any man.*
> **William Shakespeare**

What I am proposing is not some fanciful concept of my own - it is a truth known and written about by many, though perhaps experienced by relatively few. What I would ask you to try and do is put aside your doubts and try to totally accept the ideas I am offering. As you trudge through the landscape of discovery, you may glimpse in the distance, the tip of the castle which is the focus of your journey, sufficient of it, in fact, to be certain it is there. As you climb to higher and higher ground, more of the castle will appear, until the whole of the object of your aspiration is visible. Your goal is truly in sight!..

DESIRE, BELIEF & EXPECTATION

The most powerful things you have at your disposal are the desire to achieve your goal, and the total belief in your <u>ability</u> to achieve it.

One further word to the sceptic - especially if you were one of those unfortunate people hit by redundancy, job loss, or business collapse, and you felt you had lost everything. By following the practices I am suggesting, you have absolutely nothing to lose, and possibly everything to gain - and that could mean the chance to throw off depression and disappointment, increase your sense of self-esteem, and regain the control of your life. (see also Appendix 3).

There is a technique commonly used on people suffering from acute depression, based on the idea that modesty is not an attribute, but can actually be detrimental to your thinking process by not allowing you to recognise your own strengths. This can cause one to become increasingly pessimistic. The patient is actively encouraged to write out a list of all the things they think they are good at, in the form...'I am observant', 'I am intelligent', etc, and told to repeat this list to themselves several times a day, always rewarding themselves in some way at the end of each performance. It is claimed that the patient's level of happiness increases, and as it does so, the brain becomes more and more alert.

This process of building up self-esteem is of paramount importance to the process of change and personal development. If you have a good opinion of yourself, and feel good about yourself, the whole task of change, modification and improvement is made that much easier.

Please do not deny yourself the possibility of entering a happy, more contented and more fulfilling world, which may even lead to a state of greater affluence. What can you

DESIRE, BELIEF & EXPECTATION

possibly lose, other than a little time, and it could be that you have too much of that anyway!

One other important point to remember right at the outset of this exercise. Keep what you are doing, or are about to do, very much to yourself - for the time being, at least. Sharing such knowledge too soon has a way of diminishing its importance. You are just as frail and vulnerable as the next person when it comes to being undermined by someone else's scepticism. I hope you feel that you have already discovered quite a lot about yourself, and about the way in which your mind functions. It would be all too easy at this stage to allow a partner or friend to ridicule what you are attempting, producing their own brand of negativism, simply because they have not had the benefit of all the explanation and preparation that has lead you to this point in our exploration of the possible.

Your own healthy scepticism is perfectly acceptable and understandable - but don't let it be your excuse for doing nothing. Remember what inertia can do!

You bought this book! At least that shows that you are open to suggestion, and anxious to investigate the possibility of change, and to benefit from all the opportunities such things can bring. Life is for living and for enjoying. It does not have to be a constant battle for supremacy, riches, position, or material acquisition - fine, of course, if those are the things that especially interest you.

Let us now summarise our journey so far...

We have talked a great deal already about belief as all-important when considering success and achievement.

The human mind is, as we observed earlier, and in the most simplistic of layman's explanations, divided into two

DESIRE, BELIEF & EXPECTATION

main sections. The first is the conscious function that we use ceaselessly as we live our daily lives, communicating with others through speech, sight, hearing, and touch, and the second is our inner self, concerned with the medium of thought.

The thought process is concerned far more with language than with visual images. The visual is, of course, part of the process, but the pictures are always accompanied by a constant voice-over. In the recognition function, think what is happening when we tap someone on the shoulder in the street, in the belief we know them, then the moment they turn round, we see our mistake - it is someone with only a superficial resemblance to the person we mistook them for.

Our apology is instant! But consider the miraculous process that took place in that split second. Messages involving both words and pictures were flashed to the subconscious and passed to the amazing memory bank of total past experience where they were sorted, evaluated and compared, before the feed back was delivered, to inform us that we did not, in fact, know the person, and we had made a mistake! The whole process took milliseconds.

The subconscious is, just like the computer, programmable. Take as a simple example the act of walking. It is not necessary for us to *think* how to walk. We take it for granted, because we *know* how to do it. We did, however, actually have to learn the process through endless practice (rehearsal), until all the information required to accomplish this amazingly complex operation was safely stored, available for instant recall.

And so it is with every single movement we make. When we encounter a new task, new programming is required. If the task involves repetition - for example, work

DESIRE, BELIEF & EXPECTATION

on a production line - performance improves as familiarity with the task increases. Rehearsal and constant repetition produce a better and more efficient performance, as the flow of information and the resultant feed-back pass to and from the subconscious. The brain is constantly subjecting the process to adjustment, honing and perfecting every aspect of the task.

Is it possible then for this seemingly infallible and perfect mechanism to break down? During the Barcelona Olympics I recall the horrifying scene of a high diver apparently going completely out of control, tumbling untidily through the air to hit the water painfully hard. The complicated and highly rehearsed routine would have been firmly embedded in the athlete's mind. His job was to recall and *focus* on the mental picture of exactly what he had to do once he left the diving board, but for some reason there was a breakdown in this recall process, probably through distraction causing a momentary lapse of concentration at the vital moment of take off.

Why do we use expressions such as *'I'd like to sleep on it'* when we are confronted with a problem to which an answer has to be found? Instinctively, it seems, we are all aware of the fact that 'something happens' during sleep which is vaguely to do with problem solving. But how often do we deliberately set out to utilise this fantastic service? To carry around a problem solving device and not make constant use of it is foolish, to say the least. The subconscious is capable of providing answers and pointers to aid you in making correct and significant decisions. Pose the question and don't start thinking about *how* the solution will be arrived at, then quietly *listen* for the instructions that will result. Don't be impatient, for the answers are not necessarily going to appear

DESIRE, BELIEF & EXPECTATION

immediately. Just be sure of one thing - *they will appear.* It is up to you to be sufficiently *alert,* always ready to receive the information which may come as a hunch, a sudden passing thought, or a bright, clear idea as you wake in the morning. When you do get such answers, write them down *immediately.*

Your subconscious then is a most remarkable piece of equipment, grossly under-used as a tool to aid you in achieving desired goals. Think of the resource you have at your disposal! Through deliberate programming (planning and learning), your subconscious can aid you in so many ways. Most of the actions we take in our daily lives, we probably regard as automatic. But there is really no such thing as an *automatic* action - as we saw with the Olympic diver! - everything we do has to be considered, learned and rehearsed, just like the walking process. The information allowing us to do anything is stored, ready for instant recall, so we may repeat the action without having to think it through every time.

Can you accept the idea, then, that success could become a habit?

As with everything you have ever learned to do, *it is possible to learn to be successful.* The key to achieving this is simply your own attitude and total belief in the fact that it is possible. It then becomes a case of creating a set of programming instructions as the basis for what the subconscious is expected to do...

15

Planning and rehearsal

It is solutions we are seeking, not problems!

Planning is essential. Both our successes and our failures are the product and outcome of our thoughts. Has it ever struck you that people who fail do actually *plan* their own downfall? Of course this is not deliberate - it comes about through a lack of belief and the worry and uncertainty that negative thought patterns will inevitably produce.

The expectation of failure is a certain way to ensure it happens.

Unsuccessful people share one thing that distinguishes them - *they know all the reasons for failure.* They know all the *alibis* that will explain away their own lack of action or achievement. Alibis are no more than excuses -

If only I had more time...
If only I wasn't so tired...

We could go on adding to this list of *if only*. Don't play the *if only* game - and don't indulge in building alibis. Doing these things is only ensuring that your subconscious will amplify and embroider all your thoughts. Rather, use this amazing service to your own advantage - but remember who is master!

PLANNING & REHEARSAL

The power of *DE* will attract and draw both people and circumstances to you, but always be aware that, used in a negative way, it can just as easily repel. As with a magnet, there is a positive and a negative power. Which polarity will become dominant depends entirely on the way *you* are thinking.

We have all met people, who, although not exactly unsuccessful, place their reliance on accident or chance to produce results. They call it *luck.* But it has always been noted that the way in which one's luck increases expresses a direct ratio to the amount of energy one is creating through sheer hard work, coupled with positive thinking!

'All I need is a bit of luck...'
'It all comes down to being in the right place at the right time...'
'It's not what you know, but who you know...'

How often these facile remarks are trotted out! They all display evidence of a reliance on the random and the uncontrollable aspects of life to produce results, rather than attempting to create the right sort of thought patterns which could have the ability to *influence and control* circumstances.

Living by hope and accident is tantamount to allowing your life to be controlled, not to say manipulated, by outside forces and circumstances. If there is no attempt to formulate clear plans and set defined goals, without any kind of *inner* control, one is left drifting through life - again, the rudderless ship, never managing to stay on course, or quite able to see things in sharp focus.

This lack of directional thrust can so easily lead to unhappiness which, in its turn, inevitably promotes negative thinking. The result of this cycle is a tendency to become even more negative as frustration increases and boredom, the 'prince of indolence', takes charge. Life, under these conditions, has the appearance of being utterly pointless. The final stage is to slide further down this demotivational slope and, as we have seen earlier in the book, a point is eventually reached from which it is very difficult to recover.

If you prefer to rely on luck, that is entirely your choice, but remember you are playing the long odds. To shorten those odds significantly all you need to do is to plan effectively, work harder at success-producing projects, and, believe me, *your luck will increase!*

The ability to recognise opportunity is one of the natural outcomes of positive thought. But, to the negative minded person, there is, as always, a down-side, offering great scope for continued inactivity - *'it isn't worth doing that - its been done before.'*

Carmichael's First Law of Opportunity is never to turn anything down on the basis that it has been done before. Statistics show that round 300 restaurants close each year in Britain. But did you know that almost exactly the same number *open* in Britain each year? Human beings are amazingly resilient, and at their best, have a splendid capacity for believing in themselves. They do not willingly accept the idea that defeat or failure can touch them, and love to believe that they will succeed where others have failed.

There would be no entrepreneurs and no progress whatsoever if we all shied away from an idea on the basis that it had been done before. The success or failure of any endeavour depends on what the individual brings to it through personal commitment. It depends on the amount of belief they have in themselves, as well as belief in their ability to succeed. Without these splendid attributes nothing would ever be achieved.

There are two negative attitudes embodied in the *been-done-before* syndrome. The first is the implication that something was tried and failed because it was not a good idea. This allows no possibility for the likelihood that the opportunity was not dealt with effectively, therefore it failed. The second is that the person tackling the challenge was not up to its demands - or the possibility that another individual might approach the tasks from an entirely different angle, and therefore succeed. But then the person having thoughts like that is certainly not a dedicated opportunity seeker!

Another negative thought that sneaks out of those objections is simply that the *been-done-before* excuse is the perfect let-out.

Procrastination is not just the thief of time -
it is the enemy of achievement

When I wrote *Believe you can!*, this country was in the grips of a recession. Things have improved somewhat since then but there are always other countries that are experiencing a down-turn in their fortunes. These situations will not improve as long as there is a general climate of negative thinking. Unfortunately the media, on such occasions, has a tendency to dwell too much on the gloom of the economic down-side, fanning the embers of a national collective depression. It is not until a sufficient number of people with the entrepreneurial get-up-and-go spirit step out into the limelight that the chance for a national turn-around will occur. Such people can and will provide the motivational role model to inspire others to the point where that collective magic appears - a form of group *DE* - and every aspect of life begins to show the signs of moving forward again with the rebirth of optimism.

We know that human beings need to achieve and need to see their achievements recognised. The perpetual under-achiever is a sad fellow who continually fails to recognise that salvation actually lies within the limits of his own grasp. It is so easy to be free of the woolly attitudes with which he surrounds himself simply by taking positive and permanent control of his thoughts By this he would achieve some sort of focus, and be able to pull the centre of control into himself. Once he realises that by concentrating his thoughts, the object of this focus will grow, and through a process of repeated concentration, will eventually turn his thoughts into reality.

Success is not a destination, it is a journey,
relying very much on a correct state of mind.

Positive action:

1. Get into the habit of *rehearsing* forthcoming
events - and their outcome. It is a fascinating fact
that one can often influence an event in this way.
Before an interview, decide what you want the
result to be, and rehearse it over and over in your mind.
It is especially important to visualise
the detail of the final outcome, and how it is arrived at.

2. If you are a sales person, cultivate the habit of
visualising the discussion you hope to have with a
prospective buyer. See yourself as successful.
Visualise yourself reaching a successful conclusion

PLANNING & REHEARSAL

and coming out of your meeting with the order. Visualise the customer's pleasure at the purchase he has just made.

3. Develop the habit of visualising yourself as successful. Get to know just what success *feels* like!

4. Do be sure to answer all the questions posed in this chapter.

5. Make a resolution only to involve yourself in *success-producing projects*.

6. Don't waste time trying to resurrect lost causes, or in flogging dead horses. There are always new and positive projects just waiting to be taken up.

7. Have you ever indulged in the *been-done-before* syndrome? Make a resolve never to do it again! Remember, you will bring something to any situation that, because of your uniqueness, nobody else would.

16

The habit of success

From this point on, everything you do must be carried out with total belief! Not just belief in yourself, but belief in me, as well as belief in the goals you have set yourself, and belief in the fact that you know you will achieve them. Add to this, belief in the knowledge that you are going to become the person you would truly like to be, as well as belief in the attainment of all the things you are shortly to list, both abstract and physical.

Remember, all the instructions fed to your subconscious must be credible and realisable. Remember also that it is not for you to consider or try to decide on *how* these things are to be realised. What we are about to embark upon is not a process shrouded in mystery and mumbo-jumbo. It is a practical undertaking using mechanisms that are available to each one of us, mechanisms that have largely been lying dormant, just waiting for something to kick them into action. We should approach the process in a serious, intelligent and practical manner, with belief and expectation.

The instructions we are about to produce for our programming will be in the form of *declarations*. When we are considering change or modification of character or personal habits, all the declarations should be preceded by the word *I, for this is the trigger which will alert the subconscious.* It is important too that, when aiming at personal modification, rather than physical objects, everything is expressed in the present tense, as though it had already happened. I realise this may seem to contradict something I said in an earlier chapter, but that was in particular reference to the acquisition of tangible things as goals. The building of self-image is somewhat different because it is a *continuous* process. It is important that you perceive yourself in a perpetual state of change, development and improvement.

Declarations aimed at material advantages, such as the acquisition of a particular car, should be expressed in the future tense, as *expectations*. At this point I think I should clarify just what lies behind the last sentence. What we are considering is not some magic formula that is going to deliver the car of your dreams in some miraculous way. The tangible and practical objects we may list as things we would like to acquire are all going to need money! What we are aiming to do, in the first place, is to generally improve ourselves as human beings - then we will have more influence over our own lives so that we may more readily recognise opportunity, and do whatever is necessary to exploit it. It is through this general process that we may begin to achieve the means that will lead us towards the attainment of our more practical desires, such as a car, a house, and so on. But, never forget, there *is* something mystical about this process!

You are, of course, the decision-maker, but your decisions are often guided and influenced. Since the fine-tuning of character and of behavioural patterns is a slow and fluid process, it allows the subconscious endless scope to exercise its perpetual function of assessment and evaluation. Your task is to remain in a state of *constant awareness*, listening and watching for pointers, ready and prepared to act on them, for you are the locomotive means through which all instructions and ideas are implemented.

When attempting to do anything to improve one's financial status, it is always helpful to have very definite ideas about the objects one would like to acquire. In other words, it is not sufficient to simply work towards wealth as a concept, but rather to work towards the things that you would want wealth to bring you, and the ways in which it would enhance your general lifestyle. Just where the wealth will come from is not your specific concern at this stage. Your policy is to concentrate on what it would do for you!

I know that many people are baffled by the idea of these two tenses - present and future - used in making declarations. By using the present tense for the less material declarations we are empowering personal growth by making statements that focus on the promotion of self-esteem, impressing on the subconscious the way in which we expect to see ourselves. Using the future tense when thinking of tangible things we are simply focusing on objects of considerable motivational value that we would dearly like to acquire.

In the initial writing down of declarations, and in the subsequent use of them, it is important to try and visualise the way you will feel at the moment of attainment of any of your goals. This, of course, is all part of your belief. Suppose you have a real desire to lose weight. You must be able to visualise yourself as a thinner person, and to enjoy the sensation of greater mobility, better health, and a personal image that is very attractive both to you and to other people. The closer you can get to the reality, the better.

I cannot emphasise this too strongly - *it is not for you to decide how your goals are going to be achieved.* This is the concern of your subconscious. If you start thinking too logically about the attainment of a specific goal, constantly reminding yourself that you cannot see how it can be achieved, you will destroy everything you are trying to do. Why? Because you would, in effect, be informing your subconscious that there is no way of achieving what you have asked of it - and your subconscious will accept such a statement, and not make any further effort!

In attempting to bring about change, there can be no self-doubt, just *total belief* in the outcome. Allowing doubts to sneak into your mind is simply building potential failure into your plans. Once the directional pointers begin to appear, you will understand more, and realise the need for sustained positive thinking.

The time has now arrived for positive action

Let's make a start by taking a searching look at you, the person we are hoping to modify...

Take a large sheet of blank paper and list what you believe to be all your positive aspects. Remember, write these down in the present tense - for example...

I am a dynamic person...
I am forceful and persuasive...
I have an excellent and very retentive memory...
I am popular, likeable, and make friends easily...
I am physically attractive to others...
...and so on...

Make your list in the form of very clear and definite statements. Take time over this and include literally everything you can think of. This is a list of items to do with your self-image and your self-esteem. Include not only what you believe to be your best attributes, but all those you would like to think are true of you.

Please do not read beyond this page until your list is completed to your entire satisfaction

THE HABIT OF SUCCESS

Presumably you have now completed that list...

...now begin another, but this time on the basis of all the *negative* traits you think you have. Include all the things about yourself that could be improved, eliminated or modified. As with the previous list, make your list in the form of declarations starting with the word *I*...

I am always late for appointments...
I smoke too much...
I am lazy and put things off whenever I can...
I eat too much and do not take enough exercise...
I do not pay my wife and family enough attention...
...and so on...

Please, for your own sake, be thoroughly honest with yourself, and don't pull any punches. Try to see yourself as others may see you.

***Again, please complete this task
before you read any further***

THE HABIT OF SUCCESS

Between the two lists you have now made, you should have a fairly comprehensive catalogue of the positive and negative you! The question now is...

do you like the look of the person that is emerging?

How honest have you been with yourself? Have you let yourself down lightly - or have you been really tough and looked at yourself under the glare of a spotlight? Or, perhaps you have been too harsh in your self-criticism. Whatever the answers to these questions are, examine your lists carefully and analytically, taking time to really think about what you have written. Now decide...

Is there anything you would like to add or retract?
Look at all your positive statements - do they represent a 100% score?

For example, are you *totally* forceful, are you *totally* persuasive. Is your memory *perfect?* Does everybody *really* like you?

What I want you to do now is to delve further into yourself and, using a scale of 0-100%, put a rating against every statement you have made - both lists, positive and negative.

So, what sort of a person do we have now? What do you feel about the way in which you have assessed yourself. Are you perfect, or is there possibly room for improvement? Putting the percentage ratings against your answers has, I would guess, given you a more modified perspective on yourself! I have a feeling that there will be scope for at least a modicum of adjustment, if not actual improvement!

THE HABIT OF SUCCESS

Here's another thing to consider...which of the negative traits would be the first you would like to change? Your answer, for example, might be...

I am lazy and put things off whenever I can.

How do we set about putting this to rights. Simply by wishing to be more dynamic about time-keeping? I don't think so! As we know, *wishing* is no good. It is a mode of thinking that contains the seeds of doubt and potential failure. Knowing the way in which the subconscious operates, all programming instructions must be precise and accurate, for example...

I have a great deal of drive, and my energy level increases every day.
Because I am successful, I always do things NOW, and never put off until tomorrow, what I can do today.
...and so on...

Declarations of that sort put the concept of *laziness* firmly in its place by eclipsing and replacing it with a much more powerful and positive thought.

Go through your lists, continuing this process of pinning down every negative statement and replacing it with a positive declaration. Spend time over this exercise until you feel satisfied that you have a new, modified list of statements about yourself which will be the starting point for bringing the new you into existence - a you with a highly defined self-image and a high level of self-esteem.

The following are a few thoughts of my own that you may care to choose from to combine with your own list of declarations...

THE HABIT OF SUCCESS

I like myself - I am a warm, friendly, well-liked person.
My thinking is very creative, and my mind expands every day
I am enthusiastic about everything I undertake.
My health is excellent - I feel better and more
energetic every day
I do not waste time on negative thoughts or mix with
negative people.
I start work promptly each day and bring vigour and
energy to everything I do.
I am successful in everything I undertake and enjoy
all the rewards my success brings me.
I am always seeking to improve in every aspect of my life
because I know that is the true route to success.
I always bring total concentration to every task I undertake.
I am able to relax completely when I need to
conserve my energy.
I set high goals and attain them easily
because I declare and affirm them constantly.
I am considerate to other people and always respect their
feelings.
I follow up every good idea I have
and make the very most of it.
I greatly enjoy meeting people. My relaxed attitude
stimulates their confidence in me and brings
enrichment both to them and to me.

What we now have is a list of declarations that are the basis of our programme for adjusting and improving attitudes. Let us now add a few more things to the list, but this time concentrating on the more material aspects, such as income and possessions. But first...

THE HABIT OF SUCCESS

Another note - this time to my British readers!

We the British still tend to hold on to a legacy of 19th century attitudes related to the acquisition and accumulation of wealth and personal possessions! Wealth, we were taught, was something one simply did not talk about. Discussions about money were distasteful, and any show of oppulence was regarded as tasteless and vulgar.

Happily, in recent years, we have managed to temper our ideas somewhat and are beginning to accept the idea that there is nothing immoral about becoming rich! However, many older people still suffer vague feelings of discomfort when the accumulation of wealth is mentioned. Let's try to sweep notions of this sort out of the way immediately, and ask ourselves a simple question. 'If I was to become seriously rich, would it really trouble me?'

I suspect that the reason we pretend to be disinterested in wealth is because we have subconsciously decided we are never likely to attain that state - and yet, perhaps, we secretly envy those who have attained it. Hypocrisy of this sort has got to go!

In this country, until comparatively recently, we have always had a curious view of visible success, and the trappings that so often accompany it. We have been infused with the idea of work as a noble and worthy undertaking - the 'work ethic' so beloved of our Victorian forebears - and yet, the acquisition of wealth as a result of work still sometimes has an odd stigma attached to it. Perhaps this is a legacy from the Industrial Revolution, when the formation of worker's unions and the whole scenario of bosses and workers in a state of fervent and on-going conflict made the employer's state of affluence a target for discontent. Yet the labouring classes accepted that they could never aspire to

THE HABIT OF SUCCESS

ever being any better off than what they were. With attitudes like that they clearly condemned themselves to the self-fulfilling prophesy of their lamentable negative self-image.. And so, this strange idea that wealth is to be scorned lingers on, if only as a faint echo from our collective past.

Compare this view with 'The American Dream' - the belief that every citizen can achieve anything, even to becoming President of The United States of America! With a clear-minded belief on that scale, success will always be seen as something worthy of attracting the highest admiration. There is no place for envy, for the chances are alike for everyone, and success is simply something for everybody to emulate. This is what makes Americans such 'professionals'. Everyone is a professional in whatever work he or she undertakes. There is a status and natural dignity that goes with every activity, no matter how humble or trivial it may be, and this is what stimulates the attitudes of total professionalism and pride in achievement.

In Britain the arrival of a Rolls Royce in a relatively depressed neighbourhood would be cause for immediate suspicion, if not actual animosity. The feeling would be that someone was 'showing off', and deserved to be taken down a peg or two. If the car was left unattended, it would very likely be vandalised. It would certainly be regarded as a display of unnecessary opulence and the owner would likely be looked on with a degree of contempt.

If the same thing occurred in the United States, there would be nothing but admiration for a person who had so obviously 'made it', and was proudly enjoying and sharing the benefits of his success. In America, it seems that success is measured in dollars and the things they can buy.

THE HABIT OF SUCCESS

We really must rid our national conscience of attitudes of guilt in regard to the making of money! If we could learn to let go without reservation, recognising success and giving credit to all those who, through their own committed efforts achieve wealth ethically - we would all be better individuals for it. Everyone has the same opportunity to make something of their life, and if wealth is the result of effort, they deserve nothing but praise and admiration. Every successful person touches the lives of so many others in many different ways as they make and spend their money in the community, helping to promote a general prosperity.

Successful people understand the rules of wealth - the reality of the as-you-sow-so-shall-you-reap philosophy. Riches in life come about in many ways and we should always be prepared to put back into life a proportion of what we have received. Pay your dues, and the rewards to you will be endless...

Meanwhile, back at the lists!... It is now time to establish the more practical elements on our list. For example - earnings.

In the light of everything you have established about yourself - your assets, acquired skills, abilities, and so on - decide what you feel you are worth. Not in total accumulated assets, but related to your *earning power* in the world. Don't under-value yourself or under-sell your potential. Remember, the value you place on yourself will be the measure others will accept. Self-image, self-esteem, coupled with a generous dash of ambition and a lot of self-belief! - that should be the backdrop to your monetary decisions.

Let me emphasise yet again - *it is not for you to question where these earnings are coming from* - not at this stage, anyway. You must just accept that with a strong enough desire and committed belief, and the genuine intention of doing everything to stimulate movement and change in your life, things will certainly happen! Your role is simply to *be aware.* Listen for the responses that will come to you as ideas and thoughts, *and be prepared to follow all your inclinations.*

And so, just as before, write down your expectation of an earnings figure, together with a date by which it must be realised. Put this down as a series of goals, if you wish. For example...

I will receive good ideas for making money
I will be able to repay all my debts on credit cards
I will find the means to pay off my overdraft at the bank
I will have a monthly income of £ xxxxx
I will not owe anything to anyone!

If you wish, put a target date against any of the items. As before, it is important when reading through your list, to be able to visualise and enjoy the feelings the realisation of your declarations will bring. For example, really try to *feel* what it will be like to know you have paid off your overdraft. Experience the total satisfaction of knowing you owe nothing on credit cards. Feel that rosy glow of fulfilment that all these things will bring.

As I said earlier, you should also add a few purely practical items to your list, such as the car you desire to own, the house you would like to live in - and, ideally, where it should be. If you can collect pictures of any or all of these requirements (as near as possible, that is), do just that and paste them beside your declarations so that every time you read the list you see the reality.

THE HABIT OF SUCCESS

Rather than using your declarations in list form, you may prefer to transfer them on to a set of cards, so that you only see one at a time. If you have pictures of any of the items, these can obviously go on the cards too.

To visualise tangible objects is very useful, and the better you can do this, the more helpful it will be to the outcome. Really think about that house, wander through it room by room. Imagine the detail of it. Experience the feelings you will have living in it. Anything you can do to build strong images of your desires is useful. In exactly the same way, imagine the feelings that your other declarations will bring to you on their realisation. The whole idea of this process is to create a complete picture of the new you in a state of relative affluence, enjoying the life style of your own choosing. Anything you can do to both promote and enhance these images, as a total picture of your desires and expectations, will bring the realisation closer to reality.

17
The final move!

All the self-analysis is over! All our programming plans are laid, so all that is now left to do is initiate action. And that involves very little really. Go on doing the things life demands of you whilst, at all times, maintaining a state of total *awareness*. You should be listening for and following the dictates of your inner voice - the thing you might have always thought of as *inspiration* or *intuition*, or simply *having hunches or ideas out of the blue*. When ideas present themselves to you, *always write them down*. Wherever you are, put all your unexpected thoughts on paper. It is so easy to think you can do this later, but it is amazing how quickly thoughts will evaporate. It will not always be that every thought is a pearl of wisdom! Be selective, and examine all the gems you may have written down - for not every one of them will be a gem!

The service the subconscious offers is available to us all. Far too few of us use it to any real effect - we either have an over-sceptical attitude or we are too willing to disregard any help that we could receive. We prefer to go our own way in the belief that we are totally in control of our own lives, and until now, you would probably agree, that has not been the case. One thing you cannot and must not do with the subconscious is intellectualise. What I have called 'the service' is there to help and guide you. If you disagree with the ideas it presents, you are possibly only procrastinating, and that will almost certainly lead to indecisive or even negative thought processes. If you find yourself in disagreement with your subconscious, and the ideas it

THE FINAL MOVE!

appears to be presenting, just stop for a moment, and question your thinking. Why do you disagree? *Please* try to listen and be in a state of awareness, for there is so much to be gained. Have faith in what you receive and be prepared to act on the ideas you get. Remember the example of the partially sighted man, and the fact that his survival depends on believing what he *thinks* he sees.

Do not hesitate to reassess your targets from time to time, and to restart the clock. The thing you will soon discover is that goals are never actually quite achieved, for there is always something beyond that which you had set yourself as a target. Sometimes targets are achieved too easily - if this is the case, they should be modified to make their achievement a little more difficult. Try also not to be too over ambitious, for setting a target which is too far beyond your grasp is demotivating and undermining to your belief.
   So, never go battling on blindly, hoping to catch up on targets that have run out of reach. Once the pattern of over-ambitious targeting is recognised, stop and re-think the situation. A bit of fine tuning is obviously necessary to re-establish a target with all the correct motivational values. Moderation in all things! Goals and targets should be established with care and precision - but ideally, *just* out of easy reach.

All the basic preparations are complete. You have cleared out the rubbish, both physical and spiritual, and focused your attention on yourself in a way that you probably have never done before. You should now have a very clear and uncluttered picture of *yourself - not to mention the you that you hope to become!* The process we have passed through is not unlike preparing a garden for planting. The weeds have

THE FINAL MOVE!

been removed and destroyed, the ground has been prepared. All that remains now is to sow the seeds and to keep them watered on a daily basis. So...

First thing each morning, immediately after rising, and again last thing at night - just before getting into bed - find a quiet place where you will not be disturbed. Stand, if possible in front of a mirror, and quietly read aloud from your cards or list. You may at first find it embarrassing to read your declarations out loud, and no doubt you will feel somewhat self-conscious doing it. Whisper, if you like! Just so long as you can *see* yourself and *hear* the words you are uttering. The mind actually becomes more focused when the words are spoken aloud. You'll be surprised how quickly you will get over the strangeness and become used to this routine - and the reading aloud will not bother you one bit!

Of course, you do not have to confine this exercise to morning and night. Go through it any time, anywhere, but whenever and wherever you do it, it is most important to take a little time trying to visualise what each card or statement means to you. Try to build strong images - and this is where the inclusion of actual pictures has such value.

Create your own mental images and pictures as well as feeling the sensations of pleasure the realisation of your declarations will bring. The stronger these feelings and images become, the nearer the reality becomes.

Whenever you can snatch a few minutes on your own in a quiet place, go into your private *inner silence*, and listen. Empty your mind as completely as possible and concentrate on nothing in particular - just allow yourself to be a receiver. Those messages and directions can come to you at any time, so develop the habit of carrying a pocket note book.

Everything we are doing is aimed at asking for help and

THE FINAL MOVE!

guidance. It doesn't matter what or who you are asking - that is for you to decide...

...but, since you are asking,
<u>always be prepared to act on what you receive</u>.

18

Conclusion...

Let's finally summarise the entire journey we have taken.

Before any change or modification takes place there is one thing you must do, and that is to get used to the phrase *I am responsible!* - and consider all its implications.

1. *Desire*
Desiring to create change. Nothing is possible without it, whether it be related to success and achievement, or even smoking or losing weight. All things start with desire.

2. *Commitment*
Any journey, no matter how long, starts with one single step - and that step is commitment.

3. *Belief*
There must be total belief in the idea that change is possible. That is, change in one's self-image, a rebuilt self-esteem, and complete belief in one's abilities. Through the process and principles we have been following, our personal outlook on the world will be bound to change too.

4. *Declarations*
The listing of all the changes or modifications that are desired,

CONCLUSION

both in the development of personal attributes, and achievement of personal and material goals.

5. *Visualisation*
The imagery of belief. Developing strong mental pictures of all the changes you desire, and looking at pictures to reinforce that desire. To really 'feel' the situations in which you see yourself.

6. *Know your subconscious*
Getting on intimate terms with it! Feeding it problems and information. Developing the habit of quiet moments in a quiet place. *Listen - believe - act!*

7. *Ask questions*
Making 'the service' serve you in a definite way.

8. *Accept answers*
Taking notice. *Listening...*

9. *Action!*
Acting on the ideas you receive. Acting on hunches and intuitive thoughts. Being bold! Being positive! Remembering always that *this is the new you!*

That simple list summarises the techniques that will bring about the thing we have been working towards - the shaping of the new you, the person, hopefully, that you have always wanted to be.

The entire aim of this book has been to make you think.
To consider the you that was, that is, and that will be.
To create self-awareness and construct a new self-image.

CONCLUSION

To encourage you to walk tall with a new sense of your real value and your total uniqueness, and above all, to make you believe in your ability to alter circumstances.

Be aware that in the context of the whole history of mankind, there has never been a person *just* like you! And there never will be a person *just* like you ever again.

From my point of view, I have been aware whilst writing this book, that there is real danger in suggesting too much. I could so easily be instrumental in causing you to take the line of least resistance by relying too much on my suggestions, without looking any further. I am well aware that I have put forward ideas that some may find distinctly fanciful. All I would say is this:

>Examine everything that comes your way.
>Do not be quickly dismissive of anything.
>What makes sense to you, *use*.
>What seems nonsense, *discard*.
>...remember, *the choice is always yours.*

There are other ideas I could put forward, but if you have found this book interesting and of value, I know you are bound to come across other illuminating things through your increased awareness. You will find other routes to what is often called a new and changed *mind set*. You will encounter other techniques and ideas for self-development. All these you must evaluate for yourself. What I have tried to do is provide you with a simple, basic structure upon which to build...

My great hope is that in offering you your starting point, I may have been able to show you that the habit of success is an achievable goal in itself.

CONCLUSION

I want to conclude by wishing you the greatest possible success in all you undertake. If this book has been truly beneficial to you, I would be delighted to hear from you.

I hope that in this journey we have taken together I have demonstrated there is never any point or value in *believing you can't*. All that remains to be said is simply...

believe you can!

Appendix 1 - Obesity

A radio programme I heard some time ago reported on a national conference that had just concluded. The subject was concerned with the problems of obesity. The conclusions this august gathering of medical pundits came to seemed totally inadequate. All the conference's collective wisdom could offer was the fact that *obesity is a problem.* It is unfair to imply that the delegates did not come up with any concrete solution. They did - there was a concluding suggestion that the only real help the medical profession could offer was one-to-one behavioural therapy sessions for fat people - but this was totally ruled out as impractical on the grounds that such a programme would be immensely expensive, and the NHS budget just could not run to it.

I had the impression that everything that was said at this seemingly pointless happening came down to... *sorry, but we can't actually do anything for you.* How very encouraging that must have been. Another concluding idea was that the only answer to the ever-growing obesity problem was to *completely alter human behaviour and change the way society viewed the problem.* This is about as practical as suggesting the only way to solve London's traffic problem is to pull the place down and rebuild it to a new plan.

The obesity conference, on consideration, felt they were presented with an almost impossible task - so, again...*sorry!*

This has always been a classic way of side-stepping seemingly insurmountable problems - to make the problem appear so immense that there can be no real or practical answer to it - other than resorting to procedures that are known to be totally impractical or unmanageable. It is like that age-old political chestnut, *too little too late!* - suggesting

APPENDIX 1 - OBESITY

that, because the problem is so large, there is no point in trying to do *anything* about it! On the same basis, should I give up the habit of stopping my car engine, in the interests of pollution and global warming, whilst standing at traffic lights and level crossings, on the supposition that this small insignificant gesture cannot possibly do anything to alleviate the problem? It must do *something* - simply based on the fact that if everyone else did the same thing, the effect on global warming would be absolutely staggering - a matter of simple but dramatic multiplication.

There are *always* solutions to problems and it is up to all of us to just go ahead and do what we can, never allowing that any effort is ever too little or too late.

So, what can we do about obesity in the light of what we have already explored in this book concerning the human being and the power of *belief*?

Setting aside those who, unfortunately, suffer medical conditions that cause obesity, I have the suspicion that some really fat people actually enjoy their physical challenge - to some extent. It provides them with status in an odd sort of way. In making this observation, I have no wish to offend anyone, but it does have a relevance to the idea I want to develop.

We have considered in some detail how the mental process can affect the purely physical, in many aspects of our lives. The obese person could use this concept to bring about real and lasting change to their problem. Anything that could be achieved would only come about through an attitude of total commitment. Let me explain why.

It is all too often the case that really obese people do little more than toy with the idea of weight loss. They enjoy

APPENDIX 1 - OBESITY

eating so much that they overeat, and so often choose the wrong food. Their thinking is based on the belief that others can work the miracle for them. This, of course, leaves the door wide open to those who are always willing to benefit through exploiting the weaknesses of others. One has heard interviews on the radio and TV with people who claim to have spent fortunes on diets that *did not work*. They have taken pills and potions, sucked down drinks and generally spent a great deal of money in the belief that *someone else* has the answer to their problem. No diet, in the broadest possible terms, is really going to achieve the hoped-for end result, whilst the patient sits about and watches and waits.

Some weight-watching clubs come closest to generating the attitude that is really needed to produce results, because their philosophy is often based on public commitment, coupled with the idea of using rewards and peer acclaim to produce observable results.

The setting of goals? Reward for achievement? Recognition? *Now, where have we heard that before?!*

The point I cannot emphasise too strongly is that there is little point in buying the perfect diet to see whether it works any better than the last one, because doing this is based on the *hope* that someone else is going to achieve your goal for you. *Only you can expect to do that.*

There are certain obvious and practical things one must do, for instance, eat less of everything, give up second helpings, stop grazing - i.e. eating between meals. Stick to three meals a day, *cut down* on sweets, biscuits and cakes, etc. I emphasise *cut down* because there is no need to create a feeling of resentful born out of *denial*. Nothing should be too drastic. Moderation is the word, *moderation in all things*.

APPENDIX 1 - OBESITY

Now, if the obese person can handle those simple things, in the realisation that there is nothing punitive in such a regime - merely a show of common sense - there is a very good chance that results will begin to show in a relatively short time. But there must be *total commitment* to the idea, with no deviation whatsoever. The key point to remember all the time, is that *you* can achieve this on your own, *if you really want to.*

There is one thing that will make this programme work in a way that none of the others worked - *you must have a total desire to lose weight.* If real *desire* is your motivation, rather than just *hope*, you will achieve exactly what you want.

On a practical note, there are certain things one can do to help amplify the feelings that must accompany our scheme.

Write out your declaration in full and, so far as possible, relate it to a specific goal. For example, it may be your desire to lose, say, four stones in total, depending on your ideal healthy weight. Set a target date for the achievement of this final goal. Nothing desperate, remember! Be realistic, even if it means setting the goal for a year hence. Four stones sounds a lot! It sounds too dramatic. So, to make the exercise more realisable, it would be an excellent idea to set a series of sub goals. Write those down too. Your final goal is to lose 4 stones, and that equates to losing a stone every three months. If it makes you feel more comfortable, divide this by four to create a weekly target. Dedication to the idea would place this goal well within the bounds of possibility - the likelihood is that the first stone would be achieved inside the target period. If this turns out to be the case, adjust your goal for the next stone - but always be realistic - for, say, *two* months ahead. Remember, moderation in all things! Never

APPENDIX 1 - OBESITY

punish yourself by turning the regime into a programme of self-denial, or the whole thing will probably result in failure, unhappiness, and possibly, ill-health. Be kind to yourself.

Each time a sub goal is achieved, reward yourself with something you really like or enjoy - *but it would be best if this had nothing to do with food!* Make the reward something you would normally regard as a treat.

Yet another helpful technique is to eat slowly and very consciously, thinking all the time about how much you are enjoying the sensations of taste. Relish the flavours. Eat with *awareness* so that you recognise the signal that tells you you are no longer hungry, but have arrived at a feeling of pleasant satisfaction. Most of us tend to go on eating long after this point is reached, often because we have not consciously recognised it, or simply because there is still food on the plate. So, *the moment* you recognise the feeling of satisfaction, *stop eating!* The concept you will have to face up to here is that *you are able and strong enough to throw food away!* And, that is what you should do. It will not be very long, if you are able to do this, before you start putting a bit less on your plate because the idea of throwing good food away goes against the grain.

Included in your regime should be some gentle exercise, something that seriously obese people do not take to happily. Obesity and indolence are often happy bed-fellows! Again, set yourself goals. Walk half a mile a day, filling your mind with thoughts about the benefits you are bringing to yourself. Breathe deeply and try to really enjoy what you are doing, because you are doing it as a planned and structured part of your *desire* to achieve the targets you have set yourself. As time goes on, push yourself a little further by way of exercise,

APPENDIX 1 - OBESITY

but always try to *enjoy* what you are doing because it is part of what you want to achieve.

Do *not* keep jumping on the weighing scales! The constant aim must be for consistency - a visible but reasonable weight loss that is there to stay. Weighing yourself too often can become a source of discouragement. The extra exercise that you are bringing into your programme, whilst helping with the weight loss through the burning off of fat, may actually increase your muscle - and muscle weighs more than fat! Remember, it is a change in shape you are seeking - apart from weight loss. If you like, keep a note book and jot down a few vital statistics each time you weigh yourself. Neck, chest, midriff, bottom and thigh measurements are all that is needed, plus a note showing any diminishment in the figures, as well as a few words to suggest what you think was the reason for the drop in weight. To see a slow but steady diminishment in any or all of these measurements will be the greatest encouragement to you.

It is odd how over-weight people tend to congregate together. This may not be a conscious thing, but it is possible that they gain something - possibly some sort of solace - from identifying with one another. I would suggest that anyone who is *committed to losing weight* only keeps company with like-minded people, in other words, those following the same path towards serious weight-loss. This way they will almost certainly all gain strength from each other.

Always keep in mind - *and believe it!* - that, as you stick to your plan *you are going to feel quite different!* You have *sold* yourself an idea, and, as with every sale, there is a product - in this case the product is the new *you*! Imagine yourself as you *want* to be, use the power of visualisation to

APPENDIX 1 - OBESITY

keep the new image alive, and before you all the time. Create a really strong image of this new, dynamic and attractive you.

You will, of course, feel healthier generally, fitter certainly, more able to do things that have proved to be difficult in the past. You will feel livelier, you will have a much higher sense of self-esteem, and above all, you will enjoy an immense feeling of real and lasting satisfaction through achievement.

Returning to that medical conference, a possible solution *was* put forward, which was to *completely alter human behaviour and change the way society viewed the problem.* Does this ring any bells?...*if you want to change your environment, it is you that must first change!*

Remember, it is *you* who is in control. If, through your honest *desire* to lose weight, you are keeping personal control on the *inside*, not allowing outside agencies to influence you, others will notice what is happening and begin to treat you in a different way - and *that* surely *is* altering your immediate environment.

Appendix 2 - Smoking

Perhaps the most boring thing in life is to be lectured by that pious individual, the reformed smoker! I must take the risk of losing your support, for I am about to tell you how I kicked the habit! I promise you, I do this solely to demonstrate a simple point that I sincerely hope might be of help to you.

I had made various half-hearted attempts at giving up smoking, only to fall back into the habit. Mostly these attempts were motivated by other people telling me what they thought I should do, and trying to make me promise to do it.

Some ten to fifteen years ago, I was once again seriously considering the idea of stopping when I came to a very simple realisation - *I* must have an absolute *desire* to stop. That was the only way it would work. It could not be achieved easily through pressures of social conscience or the wish to please others, no matter how well intended! This may seem amazingly obvious and over-simplistic. And, of course, it is! I couldn't imagine why I had not realised such an obvious thing before. The fact is I hadn't.

So I made a definite resolve to stop smoking - born this time out of genuine desire. I decided the easiest way to achieve this, having now made the *committed decision* to actually do it, was to wait for an appropriate moment to arrive, a moment I knew I would immediately recognise.

Some days later, I had to attend a conference in Birmingham and decided to travel by train. As the train for Birmingham pulled into the station, I was struck by the sparkling cleanliness of all the carriages, obviously brand new - with the exception of one, and that was reserved for smokers. I automatically made for this haven of comfort, but, as I opened the door and climbed in, I almost choked on the

APPENDIX 2 - SMOKING

atmosphere that hit me. The interior of the carriage was filthy, with cigarette ends and ash littering the floor. Through the haze I was aware of pale, anxious faces puffing away at their cigarettes, and, quite suddenly, I thought... *I don't want to be part of this! I don't want to be segregated and condemned to this disgusting carriage - especially when the rest of the train is so bright and inviting!*

I haven't smoked from that day to this.

Now, the whole point of telling you this is because of the way I approached the decision to give up smoking, by making a commitment based on desire, and waiting until the moment was right. This made the final declaration easy - giving up was actually simplicity itself, with scarcely any of the withdrawal symptoms one associates with nicotine deprivation.

Total commitment is the only possible approach. Never try to persuade yourself that you can cut down. Of course you can. Anyone can. The idea even comes with a guarantee that you will be fully operational, back to your usual rate of consumption, in no time at all.

Regardless of the subject matter, it might be helpful to read *Appendix 1*, since all the same principles apply to kicking the smoking habit as to attempting significant weight loss.

Please believe me - giving up smoking is easy *providing you have the desire to do it*. It can be the most difficult thing to do if you are merely attempting it for the sake of someone else. Get the thinking right and the goals can be achieved...

Since it is the all important mental preparation that makes giving up relatively easy, do not make the final gesture of

APPENDIX 2 - SMOKING

stopping completely too quickly. Allow your resolve to build and strengthen towards the creation of complete desire.

There must be no sense of deprivation - rather a feeling of self-congratulation. There must be no doubts that the goal *will* be reached. If the desire is strong enough, all these problems dissolve like a puff of smoke!

It is a sad fact of life that smoking among young people is on the increase - and especially amongst girls. There have been all manner of campaigns launched, warning of the dangers, in an attempt to influence the young who are so obviously putting themselves at risk. Smoking may seem very macho to them and yet they *must* be aware of the dangers. But it is simply no use *telling* these youngsters to stop - psychologically, that just does not work, indeed it can even, in some instances, harden their resolve to continue smoking, almost in protest. Attempting to influence this situation is a *selling* job. I do not mean by that, a great national poster campaign. That is *telling*, and *telling is not selling*.

Selling is an art. It is based on the concept of creating desire, usually by showing a prospective customer that they have a *need* for the product. Once they have recognised that need, it is not a very difficult operation to change that need into a *want*. This is the point at which a sale is made. No amount of telling will create a sale (unless the information has been specifically requested), for there is a natural instinct to resist attempts at selling, once the person approached has spotted what is happening. The interesting thing is, as soon as the sale is established the salesperson can pour all the information (the *telling*) over the customer simply because he, customer, has now recognised his own need and has decided he actually wants the product.

APPENDIX 2 -SMOKING

These same principles can be utilised to sell the idea of a healthier lifestyle to young people. The most effective approach to the problem is asking questions, and then questioning the answers to those questions.

For example, if one asked such questions as...
Do you smoke?
Yes.
Do you like smoking?
Yes.
Are you aware that it is harmful to you?
...yes.
Have you ever thought you should give it up?
...er...yes.
So why didn't you?
Because I couldn't do it.
How do you know you couldn't do it?
Well, I just couldn't. I'm hooked.
Is that because you didn't really want to give up?
Oh no! I wish I could give it up, but I can't.
But that does sound as though you don't <u>really</u> want to..

...and so on. The point of this is that questioning slowly uncovers real attitudes, and the subject can gradually be lead towards some sort of personal commitment. The aim must be to lead the smoker away from the idea that they *can't* give up, and to show them that they can easily do so *if they can just get their thinking right first.* Ask them what their habit costs them. Ask them what they really like to do. Let them realise that their reward for stopping smoking could be that they have much more to spend on the things they really enjoy. This is a process, not so much of persuasion, but more of gently leading the person towards making their own

APPENDIX 2 -SMOKING

declarations and therefore drawing *themselves* towards the way of thinking that should allow them to achieve their goal - but, always providing the *desire* is there.

Appendix 3 - Redundancy

We live in a world in which there appears to be a reluctance to use honest and straight-forward words to express basic concepts. Redundancy does not become any easier to accept because it is referred to as *de-hiring, accelerated retirement, contractual disengagement, stimulated second opportunity* or simply *out-placement.*

Anyone who has experienced redundancy knows just how frightening it can be to suddenly be confronted with the realisation that one no longer has a job, and, as of that moment, the pay cheques have ceased and will no longer appear with the comforting regularity that had become the norm.

There is a sobering finality about clearing out one's desk - eyes surreptitiously watching in the awed silence as one bears away the residual flotsam of a career in a supermarket carrier bag. The cheery promises of keeping contact - made from behind the barricade of temporary security - somehow have a very hollow ring about them.

It is recognised by psychiatrists that the stress caused by the redundancy experience is on a par with the suffering that may accompany the death of a close relative or friend. It is a fact that many people go through a kind of grieving process from which it may take up to a year or more to recover. Redundancy may only be a distant possibility, yet, like the inevitability of death, it is still a devastating blow when it comes.

It is the knock to self-esteem that is the hardest blow to bear. To be singled out, perhaps from a group of equally

APPENDIX 3 - REDUNDANCY

competent associates, and marked for redundancy, can be a very bitter pill to swallow. Ends and beginnings...

In a world where human relationships are based very much on the *child/parent* roles, redundancy will often cause an individual to experience the traumatic change of stance from the role of *parent* or *adult* to that of *child,* with all the resultant reactions that such an adjustment implies. It is vital to reinstate the *parent* or, better still, the *adult* role with the minimum of delay. The *'poor me'* attitude is purely destructive, and if this cry for sympathy brings a response, it will speed the decline into morbid and wallowing self-pity. Never forget what the subconscious can do with a phrase like...*poor me!*

The very last thing that should be encouraged is a display of feelings of worthlessness for that can develop all too easily into a devastating downward spiral - a situation that is so difficult to reverse.

How well one survives the experience of redundancy depends on exactly how the circumstances are tackled.

Consider the following points...

- The greatest possible support can come from a truly sympathetic spouse or partner. It is not a *display of sympathy* that is required so much as *sympathetic understanding*. An attitude of optimism and expectation, coupled with a determination to turn things around, will act as the greatest stimulants.
- It is vitally important to act *immediately* so as not to allow feelings of self-pity to develop and lull one into a state of tired resignation and resentful inactivity. The classic dangers here are to go to bed too early, to get up too late, to

APPENDIX 3 - REDUNDANCY

sit slumped before the TV and show every sign of withdrawal from normal human contact.

- It is essential to get rid of all the natural feelings of resentment and frustration, and also the seeming insult of being cast aside in such a cavalier fashion.

- It is essential to forget feelings of the *'after all I did for you'* sort and face up to the concept of a new challenge which must be acted upon with the minimum of delay.

This may be the greatest opportunity life has yet proffered!

That, as a statement, might be difficult to appreciate at this stage since the disguise is so complete. But change is always the greatest tonic - in this case, something akin to being pushed over a precipice only to find that you have survived!

If you are one of the very many victims of economic circumstance, one of those who lost a job through being made redundant, one of those who possibly lost a business that had taken years to develop, or one of those levered out of employment under the label of *natural wastage*, I believe this book could be of value to you. If it can be instrumental in persuading you that life has dealt you an interesting hand rather than delivered a knock-out punch, I can ask for no more.

There are other possibilities for perhaps re-assessing one's position. You may have reached that point in life when you have achieved an occupational peak by fulfilling all the potential a far-sighted employer saw in you, and the only options, by way of further recognition, are downwards or sideways. You may, like the majority of people in large

APPENDIX 3 - REDUNDANCY

organisations, have been promoted to your *level of incompetence* - a curious modern phenomenon that is responsible for so much inefficiency. Once pitched into this dubious position, it is only a question of time before the consequences are recognised. This, of course, represents the end of the line so far as any future prospects are concerned. This is a point that is usually attained in any individual's career pattern between the ages of 40 and 50. What a prospect! - especially when one is aware that no further advancement is likely. There are still 15 to 25 useful working years ahead - useful, that is, if one has the courage and desire to grasp the nettle and create the changes.

We all know people who habitually bemoan the fact that they would like to have done something else in life. These are the people who probably took the soft options when confronted with those forks in the career road that demand decisions. Such people enjoy talking about the way in which life short-changed them, but if it is suggested that there is still time to start a new career and do the things they would have preferred to do, a sudden change comes over them. It is clear that complacency surrounds their current situation, slowly but persistently eroding energy levels to the point where they would prefer to go on grumbling about the status quo rather than make the effort to do something about it. There is a second thought here too - the worry that pension rights and other perks of the employment territory will be jeopardised...

Let boldness be your friend!

Change will always bring disruption, but the short-term inconveniences must be weighed against the long-term benefits. At least allow yourself the luxury of speculation.

APPENDIX 3 - REDUNDANCY

This is the point in life when any person feeling the need for change, must do a bit of serious stock-taking. Dissatisfaction with the way one's life is, should logically be the germination ground for speculative new thinking - not the graveyard of failed ambition and abandoned hopes. There, on your doorstep, is the opportunity to cast off the occupation that has become threadbare and boring through over-association. It is the moment for revitalising your life by seeking the new beginnings that will bring the sparkle back.

You may feel walled in by pension schemes and death-in-service benefits, profit sharing schemes and a variety of other artificial nails that have been hammered through your coat tails by an employer determined to ensure continued loyalty and service. But is it worth sacrificing another 15 to 25 years to tedium when, with courage, boldness and self-belief you could launch yourself into a programme of change that could result in a completely new and fulfilling career? The benefits accrued by past employment will not be lost but merely stored away against eventual retirement. We only get one stab at this lifespan of ours. There is every argument for making the very most of it in every way.

I realise that it is not everyone that can bring themselves to think in this way. You might feel that making a decision that could suddenly revolutionise one's life would be a simple thing. But there are many people who could never face up to such a prospect. We must respect, whilst feeling sympathy for, those who find themselves trapped by the seduction - albeit utterly boring - of continued employment. They are in a job for which they have no real feeling other than to see it as the means of maintaining the financial burdens with which they have surrounded themselves.

APPENDIX 3 - REDUNDANCY

Redundancy and job-loss therefore - though no sane person would seek either state willingly - may have a justified purpose if they are the instruments that set a whole train of events in motion. *The short term inconveniences set against the long-term benefits....*

Appendix 4 - Coincidence..

Some of the following thoughts were included in the general text of *'Believe you can!'*. Maybe they seem a little out of context here, appearing now as an appendix, but I wanted to include them because the remarks, I think, have a bearing on the strange workings of the mind.

Extrasensory perception - more generally known as *ESP* - does have its place in our lives. I have often wondered whether this seemingly magical facility is a left-over from something we have long forgotten, from a time when man was much more aware of his powers, and unspoken communication between individuals was commonplace.

Have you ever considered the nature of coincidence? Those odd occasions when someone telephones just as you were about to ring them! We have all experienced times in our lives when we were startled by these seemingly mysterious events. Yet, are they really so odd? If our minds have the ability to direct us towards change and success, it seems a very simple idea to accept that signals may pass between like-minded people.

How often have you walked down the street and quite suddenly, apparently by chance, encountered someone you were thinking about only moments earlier - and often when you had not been in contact with that person for a very long time? We tie the label of *coincidence* to such events. But what actually happened? *Were* you thinking about that person, or was it *he or she* who was actually thinking about *you*? Both of you were probably sending out signals to be picked up as resonances capable of response by the right recipient. Each of you may have been broadcasting your presence to the other, right up to the physical act of meeting.

APPENDIX 4 - COINCIDENCE

Your listening self could have picked up your friend's signal - and this could account for the fact that you *thought* you were thinking of your friend. The whole event and the passing of messages was so fleeting that it would be easy to have confused chicken with egg!

Some time ago I was in a large bookshop, standing in a queue, approaching one of the tills. I thought I recognised the back view of the person standing in front of me. I was on the point of tapping them on the shoulder when I happened to glance across to the corresponding queue on the other side of the shop - *and there was the very person I thought I was about to accost!* How one explains that I don't really know, other than to say it seemed to contain a confusion of messages and signals. This thing we call coincidence is perhaps more mystical than we imagine...

We all walk through life in possession of fabulous mental powers that most of us take completely for granted. It is a fact that we utilise a mere 5% of our mental potential. There are people that believe we are all components of one immense 'whole', some great collective intellect with the ability, if only we knew how to utilise it effectively, to draw on and benefit from the accumulated knowledge of mankind. A fascinating idea! However, it is also thought that man has lost or - perhaps more precisely - forgotten how to tap into this vast well. And yet, fascinating things go on happening that fall under the general heading of coincidence.

It is a most remarkable fact that inventors often stumble across the same idea in totally different parts of the world *at the same time!* They find they have been working in parallel, perhaps for years, coming to conclusions and producing the

APPENDIX 4 - COINCIDENCE

same invention, when there has been no apparent contact between them and therefore no exchange of data.

Many of the things we have talked about in this book could be linked with the concept of coincidence. For example, the whole process of making 'declarations' on a daily basis, being followed by some of those statements turning into reality *could* be attributed to coincidence. Such things might, on the other hand, be the direct result of a committed focus on an idea or an object - keeping it so much to the forefront of the mind as to make it almost inevitable that, at some point, the desired result would be achieved. It is for you, the reader, to decide what you think is really happening.

But, does it really matter? If we are able to tap into some power within ourselves that has the potential to aid our quest for change, success and achievement, why question it? - just accept the fact that things *do* happen, for which there seems no logical explanation, and be grateful! As your state of awareness develops and expands, you may discover a more acute understanding of many things that lie beyond our everyday experience.

Network & Multi-Level Marketing

(3rd revised edition)   By Allen Carmichael

This small book first appeared in 1990 called simply "Multi-Level Marketing". It was the first British book to be published on the subject.

Reprinted in 1991, it was re-titled because, by that time, the term Network Marketing seemed to be more commonly accepted - although the term *Multi-Level Marketing* perhaps still expresses the concept more obviously.

The book is intended merely as an introduction to Network Marketing - a concept through which so many people all over the world have become significantly rich, many becoming millionaires through the development of their businesses. However, that statement is not sufficient to sell the idea of becoming involved in Network Marketing. The book's aim is to explain to the newcomer just what they must expect to *have to do* if they wish to benefit from the glittering prizes so often associated with the business of Network Marketing.

This book, with its clear and concise explanations, has been responsible for thousands of people entering Network Marketing, concentrating as it does on the motivational and human aspects needed for successful involvement in a fascinating industry.

Information passed on verbally and often repeated is always in danger of both erosion and distortion, so a book of this nature has great value as both a recruiting and motivational tool. The information it contains is always available, unchanged, retaining all its initial freshness. In the development of a successful down-line, it is essential that everyone speaks the same language and develops the same habits - another example of the book's usefulness. Having been adopted by the industry as one of its 'standard' works, many networking operations use it or recommend it to both their new and existing distributors as an aid to building their business.

£4.99

CONCEPT(England)

The Network Marketing Self-Starter (2nd edition)

By Allen Carmichael

The name Allen Carmichael has become synonymous with Network Marketing publications. This, his second book on the subject, was written in response to demands for more information from people who had become fascinated by the Network Marketing/MLM concept, after reading his introductory book, *'Network & Multi-Level Marketing'*.

Network Marketing is a business concept requiring, for the success it can bring, a high degree of motivation and commitment from its devotees. The 'Network Marketing Self-Starter' takes, as its starting point, all the aspects covered in Allen Carmichael's first book, and expands them into a training course. The book is packed with useful and practical information.

It includes *The 100 days plan*, described by many as the ultimate guide to networking achievement. The plan is designed to provide, for those prepared to commit themselves completely to its simple formula, all the evidence the reader will ever need to convince him or her that high earnings are not just possible, *they are realistically achievable* - to people who are dedicated to the idea of *achieving the habit of success...*

£7.50

Please see the order form at the end of this book

CONCEPT(England)

Believe you can!

By Allen Carmichael

This is a book for anyone who wants to change their life! It is based on the simple fact that *anyone can achieve anything* providing they believe strongly enough in the possibility.

It is never too late to change or to make adjustments to the personality. The book explains in the first place why we are what we are and then leads the reader through a series of exercises designed to uncover personal potential. This information is then used as the basis for an Action Plan that will ensure success and achievement in what ever area of change or adjustment the reader is concentrating on.

The feed-back the publishers have had endorses the book's strength. It has certainly changed lives! It has been instrumental in giving new hope to people injured by the general world economic situation - people made redundant, people who have lost money, jobs, businesses. In short, people who feel they have been short-changed by life, but are prepared to do something positive about getting back their self-esteem and enjoying really living once again.

Failure in life is not just falling down, but rather, having fallen down, not having the wit, guts or determination to get up and start again...

Note: We still have copies of this book (September 1999), but, once it is sold out, the book will not be reprinted, but will be replaced by *'The Millenium Book of Self-Discovery'* (*'Believe you can!' - 2'*) - this will be priced £7.50

£6.99

CONCEPT(England)

Four-Square-Selling
By Allen Carmichael

Every one of us is involved in selling! In putting across any idea, whether we are seeking to influence others or just persuading them to our way of thinking, *we are selling!*

Marriage is the ultimate example of successful sales technique, and the maintenance of on-going relationships is dependent on the *buying* and *selling* of ideas and attitudes. The same techniques we employ in successful living work in precisely the same way in the sale of goods and services - and *that,* basically, is what *Four Square Selling* is all about. It is concerned very much with people, and especially with the difference between excellence and mediocrity.

Any company with goods or services to market needs men and women to sell them - people who not only act as the stimulators of profit and expansion, but are also ambassadors for the organisations that employ them.

The book contains a wealth of information beyond the *Four Square Selling* system itself. There is a section on the identification of personal *style* and how best to treat people of differing personality. There is a fool-proof record keeping system and a working plan designed to maximise on success whilst only working a *four-day-week.*

The theme that runs through all Allen Carmichael's books is that of the pursuit of excellence, motivated by the right ethical and practical ideas. He writes of the psychology of success in a down-to-earth manner that has helped many thousands of people to bring both change and excitement to their lives.

£7.99

Please see the order form at the end of this book

CONCEPT(England)

The Ultimate Goal!

By Allen Carmichael

Naturally what you choose to do with the information contained in this book is entirely up to you - but, if you decide to act on it, the result could be little short of dramatic. Within these covers is a complete blueprint for success, and for the attainment of total financial freedom - in fact for the achievement of The Ultimate Goal!

Allen Carmichael *is English and lives in Sussex. He has written four books on marketing, motivation and selling. He has also produced many articles for magazines both in Britain and abroad. His book 'Believe you can!' became a best-seller in Australia. His marketing books are industry 'standards' and have sold tens of thousands of copies world-wide. Certain of his books now appear in a number of foreign languages.*

Bill Quain *Ph.D. is American and lives in Florida. He is an educator and businessman and has written six books on marketing and business. He owned his first business - a hotel - at the age of 19 and progressed from there to become a professor in the Business College at the University of Central Florida in Orlando.*

This adaptation by Allen Carmichael of Bill Quain's original book, 'Reclaiming the American Dream', was written for the British market by an author totally in sympathy with all the book's concepts. It explains a system that shows ordinary men and women how to recognise the dangers of relying on a *job* for economic security - and outlines a proven system for personal success.

Here is a book destined to change many lives, and bring to its readers the means of acquiring security, wealth, and an exciting new lifestyle.

£5.99

Please see the order form at the end of this book

CONCEPT(England)

The Small Book of Personal Growth

2nd Edition

By Allen Carmichael

This small book (95 x 175mm) appeared in October 1998 and found an immediate niche in the market. It proved to be very much an 'impulse buy', selling especially well in airports and main line railway stations. A second edition appeared in June 1999.

It has, over the short time it has been available, established an affinity with *'Believe you can!'*, which, despite the fact that book has been selling steadily for about nine years, has now received a new lease of life, selling very well alongside the newer book.

'The Small Book of Personal Growth' is a summary of the human condition expressed in quotations ranging from Plato to Allen Carmichael - and a great many others besides.

Each page, designed to promote (and provoke) thought and reflection, leads the reader towards a greater understanding of him/herself and especially of the world he/she created and inhabits.

£ 4.99

CONCEPT (England)

ORDER FORM(mbsd)

Please supply ....copies
THE MILLENIUM BOOK OF SELF-DISCOVERY (ISBN 1 873288 34 4) **£7.50**

Please supply ....copies
NETWORK & MULTI-LEVEL MARKETING - 3rd Ed.
(ISBN 1 873288 14 X) **£4.99**

Please supply ....copies
THE NETWORK MARKETING SELF-STARTER - 2nd Ed
.(ISBN 1 873288 09 3) **£7.50**

Please supply ....copies
BELIEVE YOU CAN! (ISBN 1 873288 03 4) **£6.99**

Please supply ....copies
FOUR-SQUARE-SELLING (ISBN 1 873288 04 2) **£7.99**

Please supply.......................copies
THE ULTIMATE GOAL! (ISBN 1 873288 19 0) **£5.99**

Please supply.......................copies
THE SMALL BOOK OF PERSONAL GROWTH 2nd Ed.
(ISBN 1 873288 29 8) **£4.99**

U.K. (only)Postage & Packing charges: 1 book = .50p 2 books = .85p
3 books = £1.35 4 books = £1.75
Cheque/P.O for the sum of....................enclosed, including P&P charge
<u>Please make cheques and postal orders payable to CONCEPT(England)</u>
Discount prices for bulk orders are available on request

TITLE & FIRST NAMES..

SURNAME..

ADDRESS..

....

POST CODE....................PHONE/FAX.........................../...........................

CONCEPT (England) Publishers and Distributors of the Allen Carmichael books
P.O.Box 614 . P O L E G A T E . East Sussex . B N 26 5 S S . England
Telephone & Fax: 01323 485434
E-mail: sales@conceptengland.freeserve.co.uk
www.conceptengland.freeserve.co.uk

We know from past experience that once a reader
has used the order form in this book, they no longer
have a record of our address and telephone number!

So that the book contains a permanent record of this information,
the facts are as follows...

CONCEPT (England)

P.O.Box 614 . POLEGATE . East Sussex . BN26 5RY . England

Telephone & Fax: 01323 485434

E-mail: sales@conceptengland.freeserve.co.uk

Www.conceptengland.freeserve.co.uk

NOTES